D0853752

Killing lance

Harpoon or "Iron" with "toggle" head of the earliest type – a "Temple iron"

Below are shown the basic types of harpoon heads in use on hand "irons"

First toggle iron said to have been invented by a negro boatsteerer and whale-craft maker; Lewis Temple of New Bedford

wooden pin

Temple iron The first toggle iron

Later toggle iron

One-flue iron

Two-flue iron

Darting gun

Pierce & Eggers shoulder gun for bomb lances

Oars striped for quicker identification

Lengths varied from 15' to 23'

1. Harpooner or boatsteerer 16'

5. Stroke 16'

2. Bow 17'

4. Tub 17'

3. Midship 18'

Mate's steering oar 20'

Property of
TOWN WITHDRAWN GRANBY, CONN.
F. H. COSSITT LIBRARY

Class.....623.82.......   Accession.....24710.......

THE

Frederick H. Cossitt Library,

(Established 1889)

GRANBY, CONN.

WITHDRAWN

Source

Date.....March 1975.................

THE *Charles W. Morgan*

Charles W. Morgan. Painting by the author.

THE

Charles W. Morgan

By JOHN F. LEAVITT

PUBLISHED BY

Mystic Seaport

THE MARINE HISTORICAL ASSOCIATION, INCORPORATED

Mystic, Connecticut

623.82
L

Copyright © 1973 by The Marine Historical Association, Incorporated

Library of Congress Catalog Card Number: 73–83835
Hardbound ISBN: 0–913372–09–9
Paperback ISBN: 0–913372–10–2

To the officers and crews of the *Charles W. Morgan*

Contents

Illustrations

Foreword

Every once in a while a book of more than passing interest comes along, and The *Charles W. Morgan,* by John F. Leavitt, is one of these books.

The *Charles W. Morgan* is more than a ship. She is a ship on which Poseidon and other gods of the sea must have looked with special favor, because not only did she survive for more than eight decades the countless hazards of the sea as an active whaleship, but also — and equally miraculously — she was saved at the end of her long career by men who had come to love her and saw in her, as the last of her kind, a need to preserve her for posterity.

So now, almost half a century later, the *Charles W. Morgan* is very much alive and a vigorous, beloved, old lady. She has become the most treasured possession of Mystic Seaport, known and viewed by countless thousands of Americans and, to keep her hale and hearty, skilled and dedicated craftsmen lavish on her much tender loving care. She has been designated a Registered National Historic Landmark and in a very short time she will be placed back in the water in floating condition.

In truth, she is a happy ship and a miraculous ship.

Over the years much information pertaining to the long career of the *Charles W. Morgan* has come to light, together with much misinformation. Accounts of her voyages, such as *Whale Hunt* by Nelson Cole Haley, have been published, and from time to time scholars and historians have discovered new facts. But it has taken John Leavitt, our Associate Curator, to come up with much new information about this vessel and to explode some myths. An artist, a research historian and a man who actually sailed before the mast as a youth, John Leavitt has brought to this task a deep devotion for the sea and the Age of Sail, New England sailors and the ships they sail. Meticulous in his research and his paintings, Mr. Leavitt has produced a book that is of more than passing interest to anyone who loves the sea and knows the *Charles W. Morgan*. It is a significant contribution to our knowledge of this ship and the men who sailed her.

I am proud that Mystic Seaport has been able to undertake the research and publication of this book which adds an important chapter to American maritime history.

Waldo C. M. Johnston
Director
Mystic Seaport
August 31, 1973

Preface

Bᴇᴛᴡᴇᴇɴ these covers is presented what we hope is an accurate if not minutely detailed history of the whaleship *Charles W. Morgan,* built in 1841 and now preserved at Mystic Seaport as the only example of its type in the United States. One would think that a ship with such a continuity of history would be comparatively easy to research, but it has not been so altogether. Documents and other material relating to her early career seem to be missing and nowhere could we find any pictorial evidence of her appearance when new. It is known that many things about her are different, but positive evidence as to details is lacking.

For instance, we know that in the 1840s the boats were smaller and of lapstreak construction; hemp was in general use for all standing rigging; and the high afterhouse that became the identifying mark for all whaleships after the 1850–1860 period had not yet come into use. Hull decoration has been a matter of concern since so many people of the present generation are used to seeing her with painted ports, which — according to the oldest witnesses — she never had while in active whaling service. A search of her logbooks and other manuscript materials makes no reference to that form of decoration. There is a mention in the record of an early voyage that the crew had been working over the side to "blacken the bends": this would seem to intimate that she had come out with a bright wale strake, oiled instead of painted. This was a common form of decoration in early ships and was often combined with two narrow white stripes, one at the plank-sheer and another between it and the heavy wale, or bends, which was about three planks wide, the planks being somewhat thicker than the other planking above and below it. The *Emily Morgan,* built earlier for Charles Waln Morgan and others, had this form of decoration and the fact that Morgan was a birthright Quaker would make it likely he would prefer that form of decoration to the warlike false gun ports. However, while painted gun ports were a favored form of decoration among whalemen even into the later years after they had been abandoned by the merchant service, there is no direct evidence on the *Morgan* of any kind.

A mass of documentary evidence is provided by logs, journals and account books, but it rarely reveals anything special and much of it is conflicting or indecipherable. Records or recollections by descendants of ship's officers and crews are often at complete variance with government or private business records — which frequently conflict with each other. Crew lists published in this book have been especially hard to check due to the number of men involved, the desertions, discharges and deaths in foreign waters reaching proportions never heard of in merchant vessels. Poor calligraphy and original spelling by poorly educated mates and masters might as well have been Sanskrit in some instances.

However, the task of getting the material together has been an interesting one and it is hoped that the result will be a comprehensive and accurate history of the lone survivor of the golden era of American whaling.

Acknowledgements

T HE base for this book was provided largely from manuscript material in the G. W. Blunt White Library of The Marine Historical Association at Mystic Seaport. Librarian Donald Judge and members of his staff have been of invaluable assistance, as have staff members at the Seaport who have researched the vessel as well as worked on her structurally.

Photographs and information on various captains have been provided by Miss Gertrude Landers of Chagrin Falls, Ohio, a granddaughter of Captain Thomas Landers, Mr. and Mrs. Neal Landers of Manchester, Connecticut, and Mrs. Marian Church of Rochester, Massachusetts. Information on Captain and Mrs. James A. M. Earle has been supplied by James W. "Jamie" Earle, their son, who sailed on one of the whaling voyages from the West Coast. Mrs. Norman Earle, whose husband was a younger son of the Earles, has also contributed some reminiscences.

We are in debt to the Whaling Museum of the Old Dartmouth Historical Society, Richard Kugler, director, and to the Kendall Whaling Museum, Marion V. Brewington, director. The late Reginald Hegarty, curator of the Melville Room of the New Bedford Public Library, was a source of firsthand information, and Charles F. Sayle, of Nantucket, has provided several interesting photographs.

All photographs are credited to the museum or organization from which we secured them. In many cases, however, we have used photographs already in our files obtained many years ago from different sources for whom no record exists of the donor. Others, such as those originally by Whaling Enshrined, were acquired by this museum prior to or at the time when negotiations were under way to bring the ship to Mystic. Many of them are now owned by the Whaling Museum of the Old Dartmouth Historical Society. Therefore, if we do not always have the right credit line, we hope it will be forgiven. We are only too glad to acknowledge our debt to the various organizations and people mentioned above and to any others whose names may have inadvertently been omitted.

THE *Charles W. Morgan*

24710

[CHAPTER I]

"Build Me Straight, O Worthy Master"

On a July day in 1841, the 351-ton whaling ship *Charles W. Morgan* slid down the ways of the Hillman brothers' shipyard into the placid waters of the Acushnet River at New Bedford, Massachusetts. Destined to complete an active working career of thirty-seven voyages in eighty years, she would traverse more leagues of ocean than any other American whaling ship in history. When the accounts were settled for her last whaling voyage in 1921, the *Morgan* had earned a total of well over $1,400,000 from the proceeds of the spermaceti, whale oil, bone and ambergris taken from cetaceans of the seven seas. From lonely Desolation Island almost on the edge of Antarctica to the warm Azores, from the chill waters "down under" off New Zealand to the icy Bering Sea and cruising the equatorial waters of the two great oceans, no whaling ground was unexplored. She cost over $52,000 to build but returned from her first voyage with a cargo of oil and bone valued at $56,000. A summary of voyages and cargo values is given elsewhere.

The principal owner was Charles Waln Morgan, a Philadelphia-born Quaker for whom she was named. He had come to New Bedford where he married Sarah Rodman, granddaughter of William Rotch,

Charles Waln Morgan as he appeared in later life. Photograph by George F. Parlow.

the Nantucket, and later New Bedford, whaling king. Although Morgan's interests were widespread, he invested heavily in the whaling business and owned a number of vessels. In the *Charles W. Morgan* he owned an 8/16 share. Other owners holding 2/16 shares each were Samuel W. Rodman; William G. E. Pope and Morgan's nephew Samuel Griffitts Morgan, owning 2/16 jointly; and Captain Thomas A. Norton of Edgartown who was to command the vessel on her first voyage. The Hillman brothers retained a 1/16 share and another 1/16 was taken by David Brayton of New Bedford.

No name had been selected for the new ship until after she was launched, when Morgan himself was away on a business trip. Griffitts Morgan therefore chose the name arbitrarily — which did not meet with the complete approval of his uncle. It was allowed to stand, however, to become one of the most famous names in the New Bedford whaling fleet.

Today in retirement at Mystic Seaport, the ship is a monument to the men who built and sailed her, to the agents and owners who paid for her original construction and refitting for subsequent voyages. Built with simple tools by long dead shipwrights, fashioned from timber, iron, cordage and canvas, she has survived for more than the lifetime of any one man and today is the only American wooden whaler still in existence. The *Morgan* has endured everything the sea could bring against her — the gales of Cape Horn, the typhoons of the China Sea and the crushing ice of the Bering Sea. She has weathered hurricanes and River Plate *pamperos.* Death in various forms shadowed almost every voyage and every human experience has been undergone on her heaving decks or in her wake. Love and hate, bravery and cowardice, generosity and greed, kindness and brutality have inspired some of those whose lives have been linked to hers. She is one of the few tangible reminders of a vanished era when men risked their lives and fortunes at sea to build a future for themselves and their children.

When the *Morgan* was launched, whaling was at its peak. By 1819 New Bedford had almost reached parity with Nantucket in the size of her fleet and the wealth of her cargoes. By 1820, when the

Looking toward fo'c'sle head, showing ship's bell and headgear on bowsprit.

Japan grounds were discovered, New England whalers in the Pacific numbered well over a hundred vessels, most of them from New Bedford and Nantucket. Money was being made in ever increasing amounts and between 1816 and 1828 New England whalers took over 646,000 barrels of oil worth over $14,000,000. By the time the *Charles W. Morgan* had sailed on her second voyage, the American whaling fleet numbered 678 ships and barks, 35 brigs and 22 schooners with an aggregate tonnage of almost 235,000 tons, valued at $21,075,000. Thereafter whaling declined, imperceptibly at first, then faster, following the discovery of petroleum. The *Morgan* nevertheless was a lucky ship and only once in the first thirty years of her whaling career did the gross value of her cargoes drop below $50,000.

The *Morgan* sailed on her first voyage September 6, 1841, under command of Captain Norton, with twenty-six-year-old James C. Osborn, also of Edgartown, as second mate and keeper of a journal of the voyage. Osborn must have been literarily inclined for he took a library of over seventy volumes with him, including books on history, travel and memoirs as well as twenty-two volumes of Marryatt's works.

Twenty-four hours out, heading for the Azores, the men were busy rigging the boats for whaling, stowing the anchors and spare spars and setting up rigging. In those days, crews were preponderantly American with a sprinkling of experienced Azorean Portuguese whalemen. The *Morgan*'s crew were apparently a steady lot and gave the officers little trouble. Following the usual pattern, the ship made her landfall off Fayal and the captain went ashore to recruit additional men before heading down the South Atlantic.

On Monday, October 4, they picked up the northeast trade winds and bore away toward South America. Sighting no whales on the Brazil grounds they laid a course for Cape Horn and on November 1 took in the bow and waist boats in preparation for the battle around the Horn. This occupied most of the month, the ship being under double or close reefed topsails most of the time when not hove to.

The *Morgan* was a full-rigged ship with a full suit of light sails besides her working canvas. She set courses (lower sails) on the fore and mainmasts, single topsails, topgallantsails and royals on all three masts. Headsails included fore staysail, fore topmast staysail, jib and flying jib set from the bowsprit, jibboom and flying jibboom. Between the masts were topmast and topgallant staysails and on her first voyage, at least, she had spencers on both fore and mainmasts. The spanker was set from boom and gaff but brailed into the mizzenmast when furled. A complete set of lower, topmast and topgallant studdingsails were set from the fore- and mainmasts. As did all of the larger whalers, she carried three boats along the larboard side and one to starboard. (Whalemen never adopted the use of the term *port* to distinguish the left side of the vessel and continued to cling to the ancient use of *larboard* as long as there were sailing whalers.) Two, and sometimes more, spare boats were also carried.

The first whale of her career was taken by the *Morgan* two days after passing Cape Horn. Sperm whales were sighted and the starboard and larboard boats were lowered, the others having been stowed inboard to keep them from being "stove" by the heavy seas. The log records, "starboard boat struck a small cow . . . larboard boat struck and drawed its iron," meaning that both boatsteerers got a harpoon into their quarry but the harpoon of the larboard boat pulled out and the whale got away. The cow whale only produced seventeen barrels of oil but it was the first kill of the voyage and most welcome.

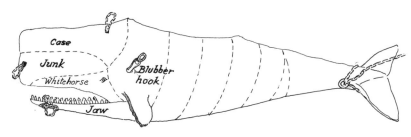

SPERM WHALE
Blubber hook inserted as indicated to start the first spiral cut in the process of stripping off the blubber. All species of whales are stripped in the same way

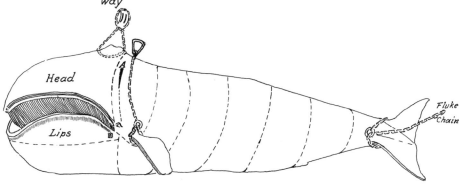

BOWHEAD WHALE
A—Cut with an ax by the overboard man to begin the process of detaching the head bone. A bone spade is also used.

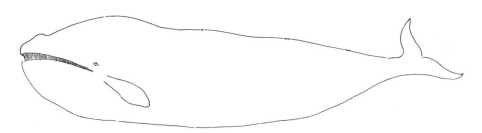

RIGHT WHALE
Cut in the same as a bowhead whale

Working up into the South Pacific, plenty of humpback, finback, right whales and porpoises were sighted, but at that time a whaling master seldom bothered with anything except sperms.

After a call at Callao for water and provisions, as well as a run ashore for the crew, the ship went to sea again to cruise the offshore grounds. In April during a spell of weather described as "glorious," young Osborn made the following entry in his journal: "Last part a fine moon to Promenade the causeway. So ends. Homesick. Lat. 2.36 — Long. 111.20." On May 28, the text reads, "took a 38 barrel bull, the first for me. . . ." Osborn was in charge of the waist boat. On June 3, a 100-barrel sperm was taken whose teeth alone weighed eighty-five pounds.

In September, after calling at the Galapagos Islands and Payta, the ship put into Tombez, Peru, where the crews from eleven other whale ships congregated aboard the *Morgan* and, according to Osborn, there was a real "breakdown." For the rest of the year they had "greasy luck" and on November 17 took six whales in one day.

Six months later the luck seems to have run out, for Osborn records: "Last part dreary and gloomy, sorrowful and homesick, sea sick and sick of the sea, amen — and it is 26 days since we have seen a whale." Other activities at the time included "building a wheelbarrow for the Old Man" and "scrimshoning."

The following entry appears in the journal for Friday, June 16, 1843: "Strong southeast trades . . . middle part about 12 o'clock a man fell overboard. The ship was luffed to the wind and a boat lowered in about two shakes. One of the boatsteerers fastened to him solid and we sterned all out of the suds. He was about ¼ mile from the ship when we got him. His name is Norton." (It was William Norton, a distant relative of the captain's.)

In August, 1843, Charles S. Chadwick, the mate, had to be discharged at Payta on account of sickness and two men deserted. Working up the Pacific, the *Morgan* called at Lahaina where she lay for a time in company with twenty-five other whaling ships. Leaving for Honolulu, they took a Mr. and Mrs. Brewer as passengers as well as several "dear little yellow girls," as Osborn described them, and after the captain had concluded some business ashore, headed for the north-west coast. On May 5, 1844, Osborn was injured in the process of lowering a boat and was laid up for several months. He celebrated his return to duty with a poem of three verses entitled "Isle of Beauty, Fare Thee Well." They were then homeward bound and on December 11, nearing New Bedford, the time-honored ceremony of dismantling the try works and heaving them overboard was carried out. The ship arrived at New Bedford January 2, 1845, 135 days out from Monterey, California.

The next two voyages of the *Charles W. Morgan,* from 1845 to 1848 and from 1849 to 1853, were under the command of Captain John D. Samson. The principal owner was Edward Mott Robinson, father of Hetty Green, later to become a multi-millionairess known as the "Witch of Wall Street." It was her son, Colonel Edward Howland Robinson Green, who was to assume the expense of preserving the *Morgan* at South Dartmouth following the vessel's retirement from active whaling over seventy years later.

It was on Captain Samson's second voyage that a seventeen-year-old boatsteerer, Nelson Cole Haley, gained the experience he was to record in a journal published in 1958 under the sponsorship of The Marine Historical Association and entitled *Whale Hunt.* (Copies of the original manuscript were given to the Association by Haley's heirs.) The voyage was not as profitable as the previous two, but it was an exciting one in many respects. Captain Samson was ill much of the time but he was a rigid disciplinarian, not above taking a rope's end to recalcitrant members of his crew, although he was not unjust and the hands had little to complain of if they did their work properly. Most of the two voyages under Samson were spent in mid-Pacific "cruising the line" as the whalemen called it. This meant working back and forth across the Pacific more or less on, or parallel to, the equator, often among the various island groups.

During the second voyage, as related in Haley's journal, the ship narrowly escaped being boarded and "cut off" by the natives of Suydenham Island in the Kingsmills. In those early days, many of the Pacific islands were peopled by headhunters, cannibals and renegade

Captain Nelson C. Haley, who made his second whaling voyage as a seventeen-year-old boatsteerer on the *Charles W. Morgan* in 1849 and his wife, Charlotte Brown Haley, in Honolulu shortly after their marriage in 1864.

Main pinrail, looking to starboard gangway.

white men, some of them escaped convicts from Australia. There were numerous instances of American whaleships being attacked, their crews overwhelmed by sheer weight of numbers or by treachery, then butchered and the ship burned after being stripped of useful gear, tools and weapons.

At Suydenham the *Morgan* had drifted in close to the reef during calm weather. The natives, obviously intent on mischief, came out in their canoes in great numbers. The *Morgan*'s crew lined the rails, armed with whatever firearms were available and with razor-edged cutting spades and lances. The natives tried to board forcibly but were driven off and, after an anxious interval, the current carried the vessel clear of the reef and sufficient breeze sprang up to take her out of danger.

Young Haley gained comparatively little except experience on the voyage, for on his return to New Bedford he had only $400 coming as his share. His outfit plus small cash advances amounted to about $200, leaving a balance due him of only $200 for the four years of work. He went on to hold mate's, and at last a master's, berth in whalers.

CHAPTER II

A Typical Ship and Service

THE *Charles W. Morgan* and her voyages were almost completely typical of the American whaler of her times. Under the old formula for tonnage, she registered 351 tons, with dimensions of 106′ 6″ x 27′ 2½″ x 13′ 7½″ and was about 111′ long from stem to stern. When remeasured in 1864 in accordance with the newly changed tonnage rule, her register dimensions became: 313.75 tons, 105.6′ x 27.7′ x 17.6′. The substantial discrepancy in depth is accounted for by the fact that under the old tonnage rule the figure of half the registered beam was used as the figure for depth in working out the formula.

As previously noted, the *Morgan* was ship-rigged when she came out, as were so many whalers of the period, but in common with most of the others she ended her active career as a double topsail bark. After the Civil War years, few of the whalers carried studdingsails, for speed had become unimportant. No early pictures of the vessel have survived, but evidence from her log books seems to indicate that, when new, she had a black hull, possibly with a bright, or oiled, wale consisting of several strakes of thicker planking a foot or so below the deck level. However, before the first voyage was over the crew were ordered over the side to "blacken the bends," another name for the wales. It is also known from log books and records of repairs that her windlass was originally located aft of her foremast and that she had a deck capstan and a number of other features different than in her later years.

The high structure at the stern — variously known as the after-house, the round house or the hurricane house — an identifying mark of all later whalers, was certainly not present in the new vessel, for such structures did not come into general use much before the 1860s. Her boats were smaller — 25′ or 26′ long and lapstreak-built, since the combination batten seam and lapstreak construction invented by James Beetle of New Bedford was not widely used for several years after the *Morgan* was launched.

At first the ship carried only four boats on her davits. There were three on her port, or "larboard" side: the *larboard* boat aft, the *waist* boat next forward and the *bow* boat abreast the fore rigging. The *starboard* boat was carried away aft on the starboard side. In later years, the *Morgan* carried five boats, the fifth one being on davits abreast the starboard fore rigging. It was designated as the *starboard bow* boat. All harpoons and boat gear were marked with the initial of the boat, that is, L., W., B., S.B. and S.B.B. Two or more spare boats were lashed upside down on the 'midship skid beams or gallows between the main- and mizzenmasts. Boats were often damaged or even completely destroyed in the process of whaling and a carpenter with a knowledge of boatbuilding was an important member of a whaler's crew.

Once the ship was at sea, her masthead lookout stations were manned during the daylight hours, usually by mates or boatsteerers, two men to each mast. The stations were formed by an extra set of crosstrees at the topgallant mast heads and double padded iron rings clamped on the mast about waist high above them. Ships carrying royals often sent them down while on the whaling grounds. It was generally customary to offer a prize of money or tobacco to the man first sighting a whale and no man in the crew was barred from seeking the prize whether on deck or perched in the rigging, where many of the hands spent much off-duty time.

The first intimation of the proximity of a whale might be only

Looking forward across after boat skids with one spare whaleboat in position. Whaling Enshrined photograph.

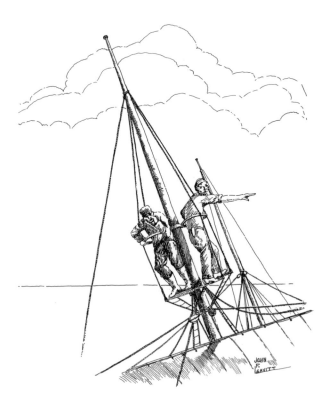

a glimpse of what appeared to be a burst of spray above the water. If it showed up as a low, "bushy" spout it meant a sperm whale in the offing. Immediately the cry would be raised — "Bl-o-o-ws, bl-o-o-ws, ah bl-o-o-ws!" Immediately the watch officer, or the master when he was on deck, demanded "Where away?" and the answer came back, "Two points aft the weather beam" or whatever was indicated. By this time, all the crew were on deck ready for the master's decision on how many boats should go. If there were but one whale only two boats might be dispatched, but often all four went down. As the hands gathered near their respective boats, the boatsteerers placed the tubs of whale line in the boats and stood by the falls, ready for the mate's order to "hoist and swing," meaning to hoist the weight of the boat off the cranes so they could be swung in alongside, allowing the boat to be lowered straight down into the water. The mate or "boat-header," as he was called when taking charge of the boat, and the

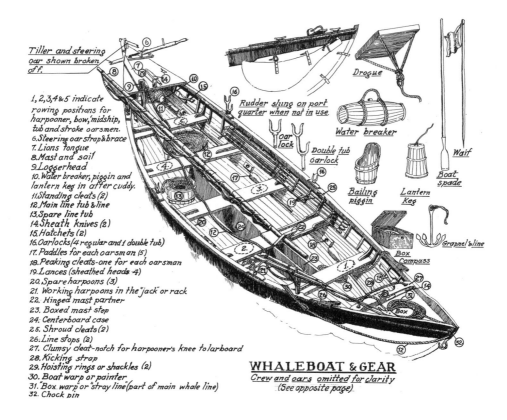

Tiller and steering
oar shown broken
off.

1, 2, 3, 4 & 5 indicate
rowing positions for
harpooner, bow, 'midship,
tub and stroke oarsmen.
6. Steering oar strap & brace
7. Lions tongue
8. Mast and sail
9. Loggerhead
10. Water breaker, piggin and
lantern keg in after cuddy.
11. Standing cleats (2)
12. Main line tub & line
13. Spare line tub
14. Sheath knives (2)
15. Hatchets (2)
16. Oarlocks (4 regular and 1 double tub)
17. Paddles for each oarsman (5)
18. Peaking cleats-one for each oarsman
19. Lances (sheathed heads 4)
20. Spare harpoons (3)
21. Working harpoons in the "jack" or rack
22. Hinged mast partner
23. Boxed mast step
24. Centerboard case
25. Shroud cleats (2)
26. Line stops (2)
27. Clumsy cleat-notch for harpooner's knee to larboard
28. Kicking strap
29. Hoisting rings or shackles (2)
30. Boat warp or painter
31. Box warp or "stray line" (part of main whale line)
32. Chock pin

Drogue

Rudder slung on port
quarter when not in use.

Water breaker

Oar
lock

Double tub
oarlock

Bailing
piggin

Lantern
Keg

Waif

Boat
spade

Box
Compass

Grapnel & line

WHALEBOAT & GEAR
Crew and oars omitted for clarity
(See opposite page)

boatsteerer or harpooner, were in the stern and bow of the boat respectively and slacked away on the falls until she was waterborne. The rest of the crew got in via the slide boards or any other way possible and took up the oars or worked at setting a sail. Sails had been used in whaleboats since the late eighteenth or early nineteenth centuries, but it was not until centerboards began to be installed that sails came to be used more than oars and paddles.

These American whaleboats were an example of perfect development of design for a specific purpose. Whaleboats were always double-ended, for it was so often necessary to back away, or "stern-all," suddenly, to avoid the sweeping flukes or crushing jaws of a fighting whale. In its final development the length of the boats reached 30′, yet their weight alone seldom exceeded 600–700 lbs. They were distinguished by a sweeping, graceful sheer and finely rounded ends, the earlier boats being longer ended. There was no skeg and the boats could be turned and maneuvered easily. They were rowed "single-

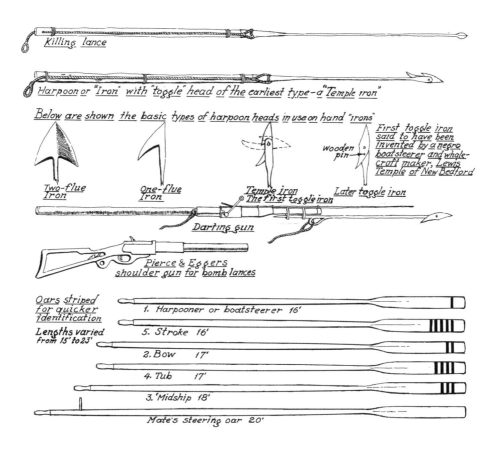

Killing lance

Harpoon or "Iron" with "toggle" head of the earliest type—a "Temple iron"

Below are shown the basic types of harpoon heads in use on hand "irons"

Two-flue Iron

One-flue Iron

Temple iron The first toggle iron

Wooden pin

Later toggle iron

First toggle iron said to have been invented by a negro boatsteerer and whale-craft maker, Lewis Temple of New Bedford

Darting gun

Pierce & Eggers shoulder gun for bomb lances

Oars striped for quicker identification

Lengths varied from 15' to 23'

1. Harpooner or boatsteerer 16'

5. Stroke 16'

2. Bow   17'

4. Tub   17'

3. "Midship 18'

Mate's steering oar 20'

banked," that is, one man to an oar with three oars to starboard and two to larboard. To gain leverage for the unusually long oars, each man sat on the far side of the thwart away from the oarlock. To equalize the pull, the oars varied in length, one long and two short to starboard and two medium length oars to larboard. Lengths varied from 16′ to 18′ and the steering oar handled by the mate or boatheader was from 20′ to 23′, having a right-angled grip for the left hand pegged into the loom about a foot below the handle.

The stem of a whaleboat was deeply notched to take the whale line, a small wooden peg being thrust through transversely to keep the line from jumping out. The peg could be broken easily if it became desirable to clear the line. Just aft of the stem was the "box," a short, sunken deck into which was coiled the "box warp" or "stray line" — a few fathoms of the whale line — which was immediately thrown overboard when the whale was harpooned. A heavy wooden brace called the "clumsy cleat" was set transversely at the after end of the box, and in it was carved a semi-circular notch on the left side into which the harpooner could set his left thigh to brace himself. In the rare instances where a harpooner was left-handed, the notch might be on the right side.

Inside of the gunwale, forward of the harpooner's oarlock, a Y-shaped crotch or "jack" projected upward. It had a leg in the middle of the Y and on each side of it rested the shafts of two harpoons, or irons, as they were called, ready for use. The second harpoon was becketed to the first one with a few fathoms of whale line and, if possible, the harpooner tried to "dart" the second iron as insurance after the first one was fast. If unable to do so, the second iron was thrown out of the boat to get it clear. In later years, harpoon guns were sometimes used instead of hand irons.

The whale line was of ¾"-diameter long-fibered manila and was the strongest obtainable. It was handled very carefully and when a new coil was broken out it was usually led up through a block aloft and down to the deck again where the harpooner flemish-coiled it smoothly into a line tub. In the earlier days the line tubs were of equal size, each taking about 150 fathoms of line. When centerboards were installed in the boats, the capacity of the main, or aftermost, tub was increased to about 225 fathoms and the other tub, made smaller to fit beside the centerboard case, took only about 75 fathoms. In either instance, the bitter end of the first line was left hanging out so it could be quickly bent to the end of the spare line if necessary. The line led aft from the tub and was passed around the "loggerhead," or post, which projected upward from the short afterdeck, then led forward up the middle of the boat to the box where a few loose coils were put down as the box warp. It was then led out through the notched stem and brought back to be made fast to the outboard harpoon. Once fast to the whale, the line was snubbed at the loggerhead and paid out as grudgingly as possible. Water was poured on it to prevent scorching of the fibers and, when slack was taken in, it was recoiled carefully in the tub.

In "going on" a whale, the procedure was cautious. If the boat were under sail, the canvas was usually furled and the mast taken down while the oars or paddles were taken up for the close approach. Boats also "went in on" a whale under sail, which was not furled until the iron was darted. It was done as quietly as possible, for a whale could be "gallied" very easily by unaccustomed sounds and take off before the harpooner got the chance to dart his iron. The field of a whale's vision is limited, and since he can neither see directly ahead nor astern, the favorite approach is from aft, preferably on the starboard side. As the boat approached closely, the mate gave the order to the harpooner to "stand up" and be ready to dart his iron. After taking in his oar, the harpooner swung around facing forward and stood up in the space just aft of the box, placed his thigh in the notch in the clumsy cleat and took up his "ready iron."

When the boat was actually up against the whale, or very near it, the mate gave the order to dart the iron and the harpooner drove it deep into the flesh, "burying it to the hitches." If possible he then snatched up the second iron and drove that in also.

The mate next gave the order "Stern all!" and the boat backed off quickly as the enraged whale reacted. Sometimes he went into a wild flurry and "sounded," heading for the bottom, dragging the whale line hissing out of the boat. Again, he might start off toward the horizon at high speed, towing the boat behind him. Whalemen called this a "Nantucket sleigh ride." It must have been exhilarating, but it was hard on a boat and more than once boats were towed off, never to be seen again. Occasionally, the whale would start thrashing in fury and attack a boat, either staving it with his flukes or "chawing" it in his powerful jaws. The long underjaw of a sperm whale was deadly and he could easily bite a whaleboat in two, sometimes taking an arm or a leg or two in the process.

Taking a whale was somewhat similar to game fishing. The basic idea was to get fast to him and hang on until he tired. A 30' whaleboat with crew and gear was an effective drogue and eventually the whale tired sufficiently to be approached and killed. At this time, the mate exchanged places with the harpooner who came aft to earn his alternate title of boatsteerer, while the mate assumed his place in the

The harpooner ready to dart his iron.

bow and took one of the razor-sharp lances from its rack on the larboard side. Once again the boat was brought in alongside the whale and the mate drove the lance deep into the body searching for the "life" — in most cases the lungs, since a whale's heart is almost impossible to locate under the circumstances. An experienced mate had little difficulty in piercing the lung and after the first thrust he "churned" the lance vigorously to enlarge the wound before backing off to await the final flurry. Occasionally a whale went berserk in his last moments, spouting masses of clotting blood, but before long his strength was gone and he rolled "fin out" — dead. A lance point in the eye furnished final proof. A hole was then cut in the head through which a towrope could be made fast and the tow to the ship began, although she was also working toward the boat as best she could.

The end was never inevitable, however, and often a boat had to be cut loose from a wounded whale, to prevent being stove or towed over the horizon. The *Morgan*'s logs record many a grim story of men killed and boats gone missing, as well as dozens of other accidents ending in loss of life or injury to the crew and damage to boats and gear.

Once back to the ship, the whale was positioned along the starboard side, flukes forward, held by a heavy chain strop which was led inboard through the "fluke pipe" — a special hawsehole at the planksheer just forward of the fore rigging. The chain was made fast to a "fluke bitt" abreast of the foremast.

In American whalers, cutting in was always done at the starboard gangway on the windward side, weather permitting. Here a section of bulwark or rail about 10′ long was removable. Just forward of the main rigging, and outside of it, was rigged the long, narrow cutting stage, somewhat longer than the gangway and held out about 10′ from the side of the ship by planks at either end. It was suspended by tackles from the main rigging and from a special stanchion forward of the gangway. Along the inner edge of the cutting stage was a waist-high railing against which the mates could lean as they wielded their cutting spades to separate the "blanket" of blubber, or fat, from the body of the whale. In the early days, double cutting stages had

Cutting in.

Cutting stage and starboard gangway. Whaling Enshrined photograph.

been used, each one simply a square wooden platform hung from the side of the ship with one man working from each, restrained from falling overboard by a rope around his waist.

With the whale alongside, the giant double cutting tackle with its twenty-inch blocks was rigged from a chain necklace, or strop, around the mainmast head. The first job was to cut away the head of the whale and secure it. To do so, the whale was rolled on its side with the lower jaw next to the ship. The mates on the stage used their cutting spades to make an incision around the socket of the lower jaw. They continued the cut around the eye to a point near the fin and cut a hole in the loosened blubber into which one of the double tackles was hooked. The crew commenced heaving on the windlass to which the falls were led and the whale was rolled over so the other side of the lower jaw could be cut away. Chain strops were rove through cuts in the head and, once the mates had cut around the edge of the skull and disjointed the backbone, the weight of the body helped to sever the head which hung from the chains rove through a special hawse-pipe aft of the gangway.

Once the head was cleared, cutting was resumed on the blanket of blubber that sheathed the body. The cuts were made diagonally and the blubber peeled off the carcass just as one might peel an apple or an orange. As the cuts continued, the blanket piece was hove upward by one of the cutting tackles. When the tackle was block to block and could be hove no higher, a hole was cut in the blanket at the gangway level, the second tackle hooked or toggled in and the first blanket piece cut off above it. This piece was then lowered through the main hatch to the upper hold, or "blubber room," where it was cut up into "horse pieces" in preparation for "trying out," or "boiling," as the whalemen more commonly called the process.

After the body was stripped of its blubber, the flukes were cut off and the carcass allowed to drift away to become a feast for the sharks and the sea birds. The head was then brought forward to the gangway, where the lower part, or "junk," was severed and brought aboard, using both cutting tackles. Once on deck, it was securely lashed to prevent it from sliding around as the ship rolled. Its weight

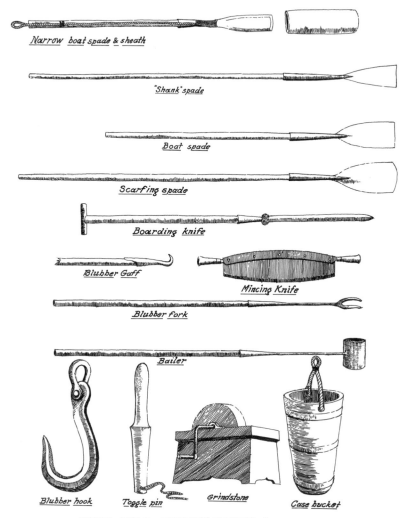

Narrow boat spade & sheath

"Shank" spade

Boat spade

Scarfing spade

Boarding knife

Blubber Gaff

Mincing Knife

Blubber fork

Bailer

Blubber hook

Toggle pin

Grindstone

Case bucket

DECK GEAR-CUTTING SPADES, etc.

was such that it could not be slung below to the blubber room and it could easily crush a man to death by jamming him against a bulwark and even stave out the bulwark.

The upper part of the head containing the "case" was then brought aboard, if small enough, or lashed level with the gangway if not. The case, in the head of a sperm whale only, is a cavity filled with pure spermaceti, a white liquid which congeals once it meets the air but resumes its liquid state when heated. It was valued particularly for making candles or as fuel for lamps. Once the case was opened, one or

Bailing the case.

two of the crew — if necessary — stripped and got into the cavity up
to their armpits and bailed out the fluid in special case buckets hoisted
out by a whip rigged from the main yard overhead. A large sperm
whale might yield from twenty to thirty barrels of spermaceti.

Once the case was emptied, the head was allowed to go free and
preparations were made for trying out the blubber. Fires were started
in the tryworks forward and the horse pieces brought up from below
to be further minced before being tossed into the huge iron try-pots.
Cooked out as bacon or fat pork might be, the blubber gave out oil
until the pots were full, when the hot oil was bailed into cooling tanks
at either side of the tryworks. From the cooling tanks it was either
bailed into barrels or run below through canvas hoses to the blubber
room, where barrels were filled to be stowed in the lower hold. Once
begun, the work went on night and day if necessary until all the blubber had been rendered into oil and the spermaceti returned to its liquid

Tryworks.

state. The smoke and occasional flare-up of flames provided a lurid scene, particularly at night when the crew, working in the dim light of a few lanterns, looked like characters from Dante's *Inferno*.

An average sperm whale yielded about 45–50 barrels of oil and a large one might produce 75 or 80. Even 100-barrel whales were not too uncommon. In later years when whalebone became valuable, right and bow-head whales were sought in the colder waters north and south of the equator. These two species produced excellent bone and large quantities of oil, 376 barrels being reported as the record.

Sperm oil was still the prime quality, however, and as long as sailing whalers carried on, their manifests always showed the "sperm oil" and "whale oil" listed separately. "Whale oil" was that taken from any other species of whale or even from porpoise or other creatures. There were other kinds of whales such as sulphur-bottom, humpback or finback, but they had a tendency to sink when killed and were largely neglected by the sailing whalemen.

28

CHAPTER III

The Most Profitable Voyage

Both the fourth and fifth voyages of the *Charles W. Morgan* under Captains Tristram P. Ripley and Thomas N. Fisher were profitable, but when Captain James A. Hamilton sailed from New Bedford on the sixth voyage he was to establish the all-time record of high earnings for the vessel. When her accounts were settled on her return, the gross value of the cargo was set at $165,407.35.

The voyage began October 4, 1859, and on November 30 the first whales were sighted. The waist boat was the first to "strike" but the line fouled and Francis Leacock, a foremast hand, was dragged out of the boat and drowned. The line had to be cut and the whale got away. The other boats, however, struck a second whale and killed him.

The *Morgan* made her way past Cape Horn late in January and anchored in Talcahuano, Chile, February 21 to give the crew time ashore and replenish supplies. From there she cruised slowly northward, the impatient young master cursing the calm weather and looking forward to his arrival at Lahaina where he would receive mail from his beloved Augusta, the wife who was waiting for him at home. His journal is filled with references to her and it was easy to see that he was looking forward to a full ship and the return to New Bedford. After a brief stopover at Lahaina and Honolulu he drove the ship for the Okhotsk Sea and by July, 1860, he was far north among the ice floes, but getting whales.

In August the *Morgan* was in Shantar Bay with some sixteen other American whalers. Here she ran into difficulty when her anchor caught under something on the bottom. Even with the assistance of Captain Manchester and extra hands from the ship *Harvest,* they were unable to heave short and broke their windlass in the effort. At last they were forced to cut the cable. Several whales were killed in the bay, but by August 30 they were bound offshore again. In his journal Captain Hamilton admits his homesickness and his longing to see his wife, but it did not deter him from driving his ship, his men and himself. He stood for no laxity and "broke" or disrated two boatsteerers who were unfortunate enough to miss when they darted their irons. In June of 1861 a bomb gun burst and badly mangled the mate's hand, requiring the amputation of a finger. With the versatility forced on him by necessity, Captain Hamilton performed the operation and in a very short time the hand was reported to be healing nicely.

By October, 1861, they were in the Okhotsk Sea with 2,700 barrels of oil stowed down. He had previously landed oil and bone at Honolulu and he was to land more before turning the ship's head for home. On November 10 he celebrated his thirty-fifth birthday, which was marked by no more than a simple entry of fact in the journal. Earlier, on May 17, he had celebrated his absent wife's birthday with a champagne toast.

In January, 1862, the ship was whaling in the vicinity of Scammon's Lagoon, during which two boats were stove and one man had his thigh broken. In April the *Morgan* was at Lahaina, making ready for the voyage home. It was a slow passage, catching whales en route, and she arrived in New Bedford May 12, 1863, three years and seven months out after an unusually successful voyage.

The ship at this time was under the management of I. Howland & Co. and owned by Edward Mott Robinson and others. What impelled them to sell after such a profitable voyage no one knows, but on her next voyage, on which she sailed December 1, 1863, the house flag of J. & W. R. Wing flew from her main truck. They had pur-

The Fo'c'sle.

chased a 5/32 interest to become part owners and agents, and, as the years went by, they increased their number of shares. When the vessel was sold to Captain Ben Cleveland fifty-three years later, they owned a 35/64 interest.

Shares in vessels were divided into sixty-fourths, thirty-seconds, sixteenths and sometimes one-eighth or one-fourth shares if not owned outright by one man or company. It was customary among most companies to allow the master to buy into the vessel and take as many shares as he could afford. It made his job surer and increased his income, for he, like the rest of the crew, shared in the profits of the voyage. The Wings were apparently not in favor of this procedure, for Captain Thomas C. Landers, who was to take the ship out on her

1863–1867 voyage, only owned a 1/32 share (probably purchased from Captain Hamilton) and left the impression among his descendants that he had been "cheated." It is entirely possible that he had been given to believe that he would have a larger interest in the vessel, but at sailing time nothing had been done.

Shares among the captain and crew depended on their status. The captain's share might range from 1/15 to 1/20 depending on how many shares of the vessel he owned, and the rest of the crew, from mates, boatsteerers and hands down to the cabin boy, would have from 1/25 to 1/200 coming to them. The average seaman might be paid off at the end of a voyage with $600 or $700, less any advance money and whatever he owed for clothing, tobacco or equipment bought from the ship's slop chest during the voyage. On the other hand, there is record of one man paying off after a poor voyage with only 10 cents, although in such cases some owners would settle for a few dollars extra to allow the man to feed and lodge himself until able to ship out again. In a few extreme cases, the end of a bad voyage showed one or two men in debt to the ship for slop chest purchases or cash advances.

Captain Landers of Mattapoisett was an older man of long whaling experience and a widower recently married to young Lydia Ann Goodspeed of Marston's Mills. She did not sail with the vessel, presumably because the Wings did not approve of captains taking their wives with them. She did, however, undertake the long and arduous journey across the country by sea, stage coach and train to San Francisco, where she stayed at the famous Cliff House until the *Morgan* came in from her long trip around Cape Horn. When the ship sailed again, Lydia Landers was aboard to begin her married life afloat and make the ship for the first time a "hen frigate" — the term used by seamen to designate a vessel whose master took his wife to sea with him. It was used jokingly or otherwise, depending upon circumstances and the sense of humor involved.

Mrs. Landers joined the ship early in 1864 and apparently settled down to a happy domestic life with her captain. He had built for her a gimballed bed which always remained level no matter how the ves-

Lydia Goodspeed Landers, bride of Captain Thomas C. Landers, when she became his second wife, and Captain Thomas C. Landers, master of the *Morgan* on the 1863 voyage. Courtesy Miss Gertrude M. Landers.

sel rolled, and a special "gamming" chair for the occasions when she would be hoisted out and in over the side to visit another ship on the whaling grounds. The custom of gamming was indulged in by all whalers and almost invariably, when two whale ships sighted each other, they hove to and some of the crews and officers visited back and forth from ship to ship. If captains were accompanied by their wives, the ladies were always eager to go, despite what to them must have ·seemed a dangerous method of transporation. In a day when slacks or shorts were nonexistent, long full skirts were not very practical for climbing in and out of small boats at sea. Many skippers, Captain Landers among them, had a chair built with rope slings and a platform beneath, which was hoisted inboard or outboard with a whip rigged from the main yard. The wife could then, while seated in the chair, be hoisted out over the rail, lowered to the whaleboat and rowed

Captain's stateroom showing gimballed bed built for Captain Thomas C. Lander's bride for the 1863 voyage.

Captain's sleeping cabin and water closet, looking aft. Research Society photograph.

across to the other vessel. There she was hoisted aboard with a whip rigged in the same fashion.

The log of the *Morgan* indicates that many other whalers were sighted in the course of her hunting and she gammed with a number of them. Young Mrs. Landers must have had numerous opportunities to socialize, although it was certainly a far cry from the neighborly gossiping across backyard fences to which she was probably accustomed in Marston's Mills or New Bedford.

Captain Landers must have been quite happy in the presence of his bride, but before long, tragedy robbed him of some of his joy. Among the crew was a sixteen-year-old son, Arthur, born of his first marriage. On a July day in 1864 while headed for Shantar Bay, the lad fell overboard, and despite all efforts to save him, drowned. Just how the accident happened is not certain, and a tradition among descendants seems to be based on the belief that he was lost while trying to go aloft during a gale. The ship's log, however, simply says that in the process of tacking ship the boy fell overboard.

How Captain Landers or the other members of the crew felt must remain conjecture, for no record remains of personal reactions. The captain must have derived some consolation from the fact that his young wife was due to present him with a child which might, as much as possible, compensate for the loss. Some months later Captain Landers took her ashore at Guam where medical assistance was available, and there a son was born who was immediately named Arthur Landers after the first son. The baby was brought aboard at the age of three weeks and finished out the voyage which lasted two years longer.

Although no doubt the tragedy of the death of the first son was softened somewhat by the arrival of the second, Captain Landers was unquestionably much affected and it seemed that troubles began to multiply thereafter. He had serious difficulties with his mates and various crew members. There were complaints from the crew about food and numerous desertions.

The first mate for the voyage was Charles W. Chace, an experienced and competent officer and whaleman but apparently stiff-necked and stubborn where his prerogatives were concerned. In his journal

Arthur Landers, second son of Captain Thomas Landers, born at Guam, who was given name of older half-brother drowned earlier in the voyage. Courtesy Miss Gertrude M. Landers.

he recounts how Captain Landers showed evidence of much shortness of temper and the two men locked horns after the captain had countermanded one of Chace's orders. Oaths and epithets flew freely and Chace was relieved of duty and ordered to his room. Both men soon realized that a capable mate was necessary and Chace was restored to duty. Captain Landers was next involved in a row with a boatheader named Sullivan, after sailing away from Sullivan's boat while it was attempting to regain the ship following a fruitless attempt to strike a whale. This led to a tussle between them. Another mate, Cushman, sided with Sullivan, as did a number of the crew. One man was clapped in irons and for a time the situation seemed to be approaching mutiny.

From then on, Chace's journal is a record of desertions, drunkenness on duty, men in double irons and a general breakdown of discipline. Two natives of the Marianas, shipped to replace deserters, fell from aloft and one died of his injuries. Later on, the trouble between the captain and first mate flared up again and at times it appears they were almost on the verge of fisticuffs.

After one more swing through the Caroline Islands and up to the Okhotsk Sea, Captain Landers headed for New Bedford, stopping for a short visit at fabulous Tahiti before squaring away for Cape Horn. At Barbados six of the crew stole a boat and deserted. The steward, who had been in irons for some weeks, went ashore with the avowed intention of filing a complaint with the American consul, but disappeared and never rejoined the ship.

The voyage, a reasonably profitable one, ended June 12, 1867, but the difficulties, combined with other factors, apparently influenced Captain Landers to retire. He returned to his old home in Mattapoisett with his wife and small son to spend the rest of his days ashore. Three more children were born to them, and through various members of the family several mementoes of the voyage have come to Mystic Seaport.

Carpenter's bench aft of tryworks, looking toward starboard gangway.

Looking to starboard across booby hatch, showing bitt and hawsepipe for head chains.

CHAPTER IV

The Morgan Rerigged

AFTER her return in 1867 the *Morgan* was remeasured under the new government tonnage rule, which resulted in altering her registered tonnage from 351 to 313.75. The yards were also removed from the mizzenmast and from then on she is listed as a bark in the New Bedford registers. Just exactly how extensive the rerigging job was is not known. Originally she would have had all hemp standing rigging, but it is doubtful if much of it was replaced since she sailed almost immediately on July 17. Some quick overhaul work had been done and the bottom had been recoppered. She still carried her single topsails.

Captain George Athearn, formerly master of the *Emily Morgan*, was in command and he spent the month of August and part of September cruising the whaling grounds off the Azores. The hasty fitting out of the vessel resulted in a number of minor failures in the rigging, including the breaking of the main yard truss and the necessity for fitting spreaders to take the topgallant and royal backstays. Some men deserted and others were recruited. They had very little luck, however, and were well down in the Atlantic before the first whales were raised. The larboard, waist and bow boats each struck and killed, although the waist boat was capsized in the process. The ship rounded Cape Horn November 27 and spent the first of 1868 cruising off the

Chilean coast. On March 1 they anchored at San Carlo where twelve men promptly deserted. The *Morgan* got to sea once more on March 16 and for the next couple of months worked her way slowly across the Pacific.

In June she was cruising off the Marquesas Islands, made famous in Herman Melville's *Typee.* Captain Athearn had developed a badly ulcerated ankle and in July, with Tahiti in sight, he decided to seek medical assistance ashore. The ship was left in charge of mate Alvan H. Davis. The attractions of Tahiti proved too much for some of the men and six of them deserted. Only three natives could be found as replacements, but once the vessel was at sea three stowaways appeared and were pressed into service. In September the *Morgan* returned to Tahiti and two of the previous deserters returned voluntarily. By September 10 the French police had picked up the rest of the runaways and the log records, "gave the two ringleaders one dozen each," which could only mean a rope's end across their backs, despite the fact that flogging had been made illegal in American ships many years before.

October of 1869 found the *Morgan* cruising off New Zealand, but before the New Year of 1870 she was back off the Chilean coast. It was good for the captain and most of the crew of the Boston ship *Sunbeam* that they were, for on April 1, 1870, the *Sunbeam,* eighteen days out of Iquique bound for Boston, caught fire and sank within two hours, taking six of her crew with her. The masthead men aboard the *Morgan* had sighted the smoke at about noon and at first thought it was another whaler "boiling." But as the smoke grew thicker and mounted higher, the captain changed course and the *Morgan* headed off to investigate. At 2 P.M. they came upon one boat containing Captain John Chadwick, his son and eleven of the crew. They were picked up and taken in to Talcahuano.

In October the *Morgan* came upon another disaster when she fell in with the Italian bark *Cincinatte,* of Genoa, loaded with guano and in a sinking condition. She had been abandoned some time previously, although there was no sign of the boats. Some sails and gear were stripped from her and the derelict shortly sank.

In December Captain Athearn decided to head for home and the *Morgan* was kept off to make the Cape Horn passage. She passed the Horn December 29 and for several days was under reefed topsails and other storm canvas.

Death was still shadowing the ship, for on Wednesday, January 25, 1871, the handwriting in the log changes abruptly and records: "At 6, Mr. Davis, the mate, was taken very sudden with heart disease he died immediately and never spoke a word at 8 p.m. laid him out middle part blowing fresh . . . employed making a coffin. . . ."

Thursday, February 2, 1871, ". . . latter part the same with foggy weather got the coffin up and put it under the boat on the house set the course, jib, and spanker so ends." The dead mate was Alvan H. Davis of Mattapoisett, Massachusetts, an experienced whaleman although a comparatively young man. His place was taken by Frederick Swain, the second mate. The entries recounting the death of the second most important officer aboard were typical of the way logs were kept. The ship and her welfare were of primary importance and the fate of the men who manned her was mentioned always in the second order of things. In many instances the death of a shipmate probably affected the rest of the ship's company deeply, but one would never know it from the records in most of the logs.

The ship worked slowly up the Atlantic and on August 14 the time honored "end of the voyage" ceremony was carried out by tearing down the brick tryworks and throwing the bricks overboard. The tryworks on a whaler are built over a "goose pen," a watertight box fitted on the deck and kept filled with water to prevent the possibility of the deck catching fire from the heat of the tryworks when in use. Unless opened up and aired out periodically, the deck tended to rot, so a new tryworks was built at the beginning of each voyage.

The *Morgan* reached New Bedford August 16, the total catch being valued at just under $50,000.

For the ninth voyage Captain John M. Tinkham broke the previous pattern by rounding the Cape of Good Hope to whaling grounds off Madagascar and Mauritius in the Indian Ocean. This voyage was a very successful one and more or less without incident. Hiram W.

Outboard profile, drawn by Robert C. Allyn, Seaport technical staff.

Look, the young steward who had been in the *Morgan* under Captain Athearn, kept a journal and described some amusing "social affairs" ashore involving the black "royal family" of the king of Antigonil on the east coast of Madagascar. The voyage lasted three years and one month and ended at New Bedford October 31, 1874, showing a gross oil and bone value of just under $79,000.

That winter the *Morgan* was extensively refitted. The work included new bulwarks, new fore and main channels and new bowsprit bitts. The hull was stripped, caulked and recoppered and several new spars made and installed. Some new wire rigging was installed, including new headstays, bowsprit guys and topmast rigging. New lanyards were rove off for shrouds and backstays.

She sailed once more April 23, 1875, with Captain Tinkham again in command, hoping to repeat the success of his previous voyage. His young wife accompanied him and he made special provision for her benefit, even building a small deckhouse to provide far better light and air than the rather cramped, musty quarters below decks. Unfortunately she suffered from severe bouts of seasickness and finally was put ashore at Durban, where she took a steamer to England and thence home. After finishing another voyage of more than three years duration, the *Morgan* arrived back at New Bedford May 17, 1878, with a cargo of oil and bone valued at less than a third of the previous voyage. Captain Tinkham apparently decided that further whaling was not for him and retired to a farm just outside New Bedford.

Two months elapsed before the *Morgan* was ready for sea again. In the meantime, general repairs were made, the topsides recaulked and the bottom recoppered. New fore- and mainmasts and a new bowsprit were installed, all having been shortened three feet. A new main topsail yard and a new main topgallant mast replaced older spars, while new fore topmast backstays and new martingale guys were fitted.

Captain Thomas Ellis took her out in July and headed for the western grounds near the Azores. In late August he sailed southward to the Cape Verdes and from there worked down to St. Helena. He spent practically the entire voyage whaling in the area around that island and arrived at New Bedford May 11, 1881, with a cargo of oil and bone worth $52,486.60.

Looking forward on starboard side to fo'c'sle head, windlass, companionway to crew's quarters, and fluke bitt beside mast. Marine Research photograph.

Looking to starboard, showing windlass at left, mast and fo'c'sle companionway at right.

44

CHAPTER V

The Longest Voyage

ALTHOUGH she laid over less than two months, the vessel underwent further refitting and modernization for the next voyage. Her bottom was stripped, caulked and sheathed once more, some decking renewed and the rest completely recaulked. Ceiling in the lower hold was refastened, all copper butt bolts were examined and replaced where necessary and the hull put in perfect order. An 8″ shoe was put on the keel and new coamings were built around the fore hatch. The windlass was moved forward of the foremast from its original position aft of the mast and presumably the forecastle companionway moved to the space vacated. A new bowsprit, main yard, two main topsail yards, new fore topgallant mast and new spanker boom were added. New fore and main topmast shrouds, new fore topmast backstays and new wire forestay and jibstay were also fitted. When the vessel sailed July 13, 1881, she set double topsails on the main and a single topsail on the fore, although during the voyage an upper topsail yard was shaped and the big single topsail made into two sails. She still set royals on both fore- and mainmasts but the yards were sent down when on the whaling grounds.

As usual, Captain Charles F. Keith made for the western grounds off the Azores, but had very little luck, either in catching whales or keeping his crew pacified. Serious trouble first made its appearance

November 17 when about 4:20 in the morning James Howland, fourth officer, came running below to say the ship was on fire in the forehold. Kerosene had been spilled out from a keg and there were burned matches and burned oakum to indicate the fire had been set deliberately. Fortunately the blaze did not have enough of a start and it was soon put out. Further investigation revealed that Lawrence and Jose Correa had seen two other green hands, Harry Wilson and William Morey, removing the fore hatch and then replacing it when they saw they were being watched. Jose Correa, suspecting something was wrong, went down to the forecastle and found a knothole which allowed him to see into the hold. After a time Wilson and Morey came down and he saw them start the fire. It was also remembered that the steward, George Yale, had been seen in close conversation with the pair the previous evening, so all three men were put in irons for safekeeping.

At Brava in the Cape Verdes a tragic accident took the life of James Howland. He and William Keith, the captain's younger brother, were lowering the starboard boat to go ashore when the after davit broke, throwing both men into the water. An oar was thrown to them, but Howland slipped away and was drowned although Keith, who could swim, did his best to save him. The starboard boat was cleared but its painter parted and the boat was also lost.

Two days later Captain Keith shipped a new boatsteerer, Antone Edwards, to replace Howland. It is believed that he may have been the man by the same name who was later master of a number of New Bedford whalers, including the bark *Wanderer* at the time of her loss in 1925.

Captain Keith did not attempt the Cape Horn passage but worked around the Cape of Good Hope at the southern tip of Africa. He met with heavy weather off the Crozets and sustained considerable damage, including the breaking of another davit and the loss of the waist boat. By May 28, 1882, the vessel was anchored in Monganui Harbor, New Zealand where wood, water and provisions were obtained. Several men deserted but were taken by the natives and returned to the ship.

The *Morgan* beginning a voyage. Boat has rowed guests ashore and will be taken up on midship davits. Captain John Parker Samuels Collection at Mystic Seaport.

The year 1883 found the *Morgan* whaling in the vicinity of Chatham Island, Pitts' Island and French Rock, east and north of New Zealand, often in company with the barks *Alaska* and *Splendid*. In June the vessel returned to Monganui for provisions, anchoring with the New Bedford whalers *Adeline Gibbs* and *California*. Again there were desertions, but the men were captured and brought aboard in irons until the ship went to sea July 15.

At this time the log notes that the carpenter is engaged in making a new topsail yard and the crew reeving off new lower topsail braces, indicating a complete changeover to the full double topsail rig. The big single fore topsail was recut, making upper and lower topsails out of it. A succession of heavy gales in August, September and October kept the bark under bare poles much of the time and made whaling impossible. Earl Russell, a foremast hand, died of typhoid fever and was buried at sea November 28, and not many days later the captain came down with a fever. From January 2 through 4 the ship was cruising off the Chathams under bare poles again, with the barometer a tenth below 29. Captain Keith was still ill and on January 31 he went ashore at Pitts' Island. Apparently Mrs. Keith and their son were aboard, for at this time there is the first mention of them in the log. The captain was well enough to return to the *Morgan* by February 7 while Mrs. Keith and the boy remained ashore. They rejoined the bark in July but there is no indication that they finished the voyage. It is believed they went home by steamer, for there are no further references to them in the log and none in the Whaleman's Shipping List when the ship arrived at New Bedford.

The rest of the voyage was a tale of a few whales, many repeated desertions every time she put in at the New Zealand ports, bad weather and another death among the crew. Robert Craig, who had become steward following the desertion of George Yale, died of Bright's disease on April 12, 1885, and was buried at sea the next day.

The situation did not improve in 1886 and on March 1 Captain Keith squared away for Cape Horn and home. As if in parting salute, a westerly gale overtook the *Morgan* and on March 24 a huge sea was shipped over the stern which smashed the wheel and played hob about the decks. She had been running under lower topsails and foresail but was immediately hove to under bare poles and steps were taken to repair the wheel. The job was finished by the next day and once more the ship was back on her course under topsails, but it had been a close call. Cape Horn was passed April 2 and Bermuda, June 8. June 14 the tryworks were torn apart, the bricks thrown overboard and the cutting tackle was rigged down. Ironically, the next day a sperm whale was sighted, the boats lowered and he was killed. It was therefore necessary to rerig the cutting tackles and the whale was cut up and minced, the blubber being stowed down in casks. The lightship off Newport was made on June 17 and a pilot taken off the Hens & Chickens the same day. On June 18 the *Morgan* sailed in past Clark's Point light at New Bedford — the longest and least rewarding voyage up to that time had ended.

CHAPTER VI

Through the Golden Gate

BEGINNING in 1886, when she sailed October 6 from New Bedford, another drastic change was made in the pattern of voyages. It was the last time she was to see her hailing port for more than eighteen years. Although sperm oil was still considered to be of premium grade, bringing a somewhat higher price, sperm whales were nowhere near as numerous as they had been in earlier years. During the last two decades of the nineteenth century, more and more whalemen were beginning to depend upon the catches of right and bowhead whales for the greatest overall profit. Whalebone became more valuable as well and these two species were generous suppliers. The Japan grounds, the Okhotsk Sea off the Russian coast and the Bering Sea were the favored hunting grounds, but since they could be worked only during comparatively good weather the voyages were seldom of more than a year's duration. The whaling fleet therefore changed its base to San Francisco, thus avoiding the long journey from home ports on the East Coast to whaling grounds around Cape Horn to the west.

In fitting out for this voyage, the *Morgan* underwent numerous changes. Her hull was checked over carefully and some new 'tween deck knees were installed. She was refastened wherever any looseness was indicated and the bow reinforced in preparation for encounters with arctic ice. Her stern was extensively rebuilt and it has been widely

Stern view of *Morgan* hauled out for work on bottom. Courtesy Kendall Whaling Museum.

assumed that this was when her stern windows were removed and two small, round ports substituted. On the other hand, Captain James Earle, who picked up several escaped Russian prisoners in 1893, mentions specifically in his account of the incident how the sharp stem of the sampan from which they were taken stove in one of the stern windows when the small craft came up on a swell while lying astern of the bark on a line.

A steam deck engine was also installed forward and a small deckhouse built to go on the main deck under the after skid beams. This became the galley.

Captain George A. Smith, formerly mate in the vessel, took command. He headed for the Pacific and spent about three months cruising in the vicinity of Norfolk Island and Guam before steering for the Japan grounds and the Okhotsk Sea. The *Morgan* made port at San Francisco November 4, 1887, one month over a year at sea with a cargo valued at more than $50,000.

By December 3, 1887, she had refitted and sailed under Captain Smith again, working the same grounds. This time he was not so lucky, however, and when he returned to San Francisco November 5, 1888, his cargo was valued at less than $20,000.

Captain John S. Layton took her out on the next two voyages, doing very well on the first but only half as well on the second. Just before starting back for San Francisco from the second voyage, the larboard boat in charge of the second mate, Honorio Martin, chased a big 100-barrel bull which, after being harpooned, towed them off on a Nantucket sleigh ride. When the boat finally got close enough for the mate to lance and kill the whale, the *Morgan* was out of sight with night coming on. The mate decided to lay by the whale all night, believing that the ship would appear in the morning, but sunup showed no trace of her on the horizon. It soon became evident that the *Morgan* had lost all track of them and with only a few emergency supplies of food and water they regretfully decided to leave the whale and make for the coast of Saghalin Island, known to be about 100 miles west. The boat was under sail and the near-starving men finally got ashore five days later. They started inland to search for assistance

Property of the TOWN OF GRANBY, CONN. F. H. COSSITT LIBRARY

24710

and returned just in time to see the *Charles W. Morgan* sailing away, ending a search for them. Some natives gave them fish to eat and water to drink and then guided them to the nearest Russian settlement, which turned out to be a convict camp. Suspected of being spies by the Russians, it took some time to gain their release and reach Hong Kong, where they took passage on a steamer for San Francisco. They arrived there December 7, more than a month after the *Morgan* had returned and reported them lost. This adventure was to have something of a sequel three years later when, under command of Captain James A. M. Earle, the vessel was cruising for whales in about the same waters.

On September 10, 1893, a lookout aloft on the *Morgan* sighted a strange craft making for the ship and hailed the deck with the information. Captain Earle took a glass aloft and spotted a crude sampan with ten men aboard. Obviously they were not Japanese fishermen and Earle's suspicions made him go down to his cabin for a revolver. When he came on deck he told the mate to take their line if they came alongside but not to allow them aboard. They finally reached the *Morgan,* making signs indicating hunger and thirst. Dressed in ragged odds and ends of clothing, they presented a wild appearance. A member of the whaler's crew native to the Pribiloff Islands spoke with them and it was soon revealed that they were Russian prisoners from the same camp which the *Morgan*'s boat crew had reached three years earlier. It was nothing more than coincidence, of course, but an interesting one. The escapees had finished the last of their food and water several days before and the sampan was showing signs of breaking up as she pitched and rolled at the end of the *Morgan*'s line. At one point, the long overhanging bow, rising on a swell beneath the stern, stove in one of the cabin windows and Captain Earle decided that the only thing he could do was take the men aboard, cast the sampan adrift and proceed on his way. A few days later they fell in with the bark *Cape Horn Pigeon* commanded by Captain Thomas Scullun, an old friend, who was persuaded to take five of the men aboard his vessel.

Upon returning to San Francisco Captain Earle reported to the authorities, but due to the unusual aspects of the case no one seemed to want to become involved. For a time the escapees were taken in hand by an entrepreneur who exhibited them in a dime museum show, but eventually they broke up and went their separate ways. Three of them were involved in killing a farmer and then two of them turned on the third and killed him. They were apprehended and hanged and the rest of the former convicts were absorbed into American life.

Captain Earle had taken over the *Charles W. Morgan* in 1890 following Layton's return from his second voyage. He was widely known in the whaling fleet, primarily for his good fortune as master of the bark *Splendid* in taking a whale which yielded over $150,000 worth of ambergris. He was a native of Martha's Vineyard and had begun his whaling career at the age of twelve in the old bark *Europa*. Starting as a boy, he rose through the grades of foremast hand, harpooner and boatsteerer, to mate and master. He was not only competent but also had the reputation of being lucky. Much of his "luck" was the result of forethought and careful study of whales and whaling grounds. He retained command of the *Morgan* for five years until 1896. On the last voyage of the five, he called at Honolulu in January and, at the home of friends there, was married to Miss Honor Matthews, a New Zealand school teacher whom he had met at Russell, New Zealand. They had corresponded and Miss Matthews came up by steamer and met him at Honolulu for the ceremony. They sailed immediately on their seagoing honeymoon and Mrs. Earle soon showed she could be at home afloat as well as ashore. She learned navigation and was admired and respected by all the crews of her husband's ships. That particular voyage ended at San Francisco November 6, 1896, and Earle handed the ship back to Captain Layton while he took his bride east by train.

Captain Earle was lucky with the *Morgan*. He seemed to have less crew trouble than many masters and was blessed with some excellent mates and petty officers. In 1894, the mate, Frederick C. Swain, a Nantucketer and a whaleman of long experience, was killed when his boat went in on a big bull sperm on the New Zealand grounds. Captain Earle was watching through the glasses and saw the boat reach the monster and the harpooner dart the iron. The whale exploded immediately into a frenzy of action and one sweep of his giant flukes stove the boat to kindling wood, leaving the crew struggling in the water. The other boats pulled in to the rescue and picked up five men. Swain's hat floating on the water told the grim story and wreckage from the boat indicated that the flukes had struck the stern first and probably killed him as he stood at the tiller. Ironically, this was to have been his last trip and Captain Earle was grieved to see a good man lost under such circumstances.

Another favorite of Earle's was Emanuel Morgan, a native of the Seychelle Islands. A very competent whaleman, he was widely known in the whaling fleet, but English was not his native tongue and his recording of events in the *Morgan*'s various log books was laconic and ultra simple in content, punctuation and spelling. Earle also thought very well of Richard McLachlan of New Zealand, a young third mate of the *Morgan,* and later expressed much regret when he heard of his death at an early age. McLachlan was the model for the harpooner in the famous Bela Pratt bronze, "A Dead Whale or a Stove Boat," which stands in front of the New Bedford Public Library. A most reliable second officer in Earle's estimation was George Parkin Christian of Norfolk Island, great-grandson of Fletcher Christian, leader of the *Bounty* mutineers.

After taking over from Earle, Captain Layton made a single voyage in 1896–97 and then relinquished command to Captain Thomas Scullun, late of the *Cape Horn Pigeon,* lost near Hakodate, Japan, just previously. In fact, Captain Layton had purchased boats and gear from the wreck as well as signing four men from the crew and Emanuel Morgan, one of the mates, as boatheader.

Captain Scullun remained with the *Morgan* for the 1898–99 and 1899–1900 voyages with consistently good returns on his cargoes, then turned her back to Earle again in 1900. By this time the voyages were almost routine. Leaving San Francisco, the vessel was usually headed for the mid-Pacific area until warmer weather, when she sailed for the Okhotsk Sea and the northern waters after right and bowhead whales.

George Parkin Christian, left, great-grandson of Fletcher Christian of *Bounty* mutineers, was boatsteerer, second mate and mate for many years on *Morgan*. Other crew member is 4th mate Antone Alameda. Courtesy H. H. Kynett.

James Earle made a successful voyage with the *Morgan* from November 1900 to October 1901 and upon the return to San Francisco Captain Scullun took over again for a voyage. By this time, Emanuel Morgan was chief mate and log keeper.

The 1901–02 voyage was fairly uneventful but quite profitable. At one time the log records that one day they had nine sperm whales alongside waiting to be cut in and five on two other occasions. One man fell from aloft while painting the lower masts and sustained a compound fracture of a leg which left him crippled for the rest of his life. He was Nelson Lambert, a native of Guadeloupe in the West Indies. After leaving the *Morgan* he settled in Providence and on several occasions before his death visited the old ship at South Dartmouth and Mystic. He was inclined to feel rather bitter about the accident, claiming that he had not received proper care, with the result that he became permanently disabled. Knowledge of medicine and surgery was quite rudimentary among the officers and crews of whalers, and at the time the accident took place there was apparently no nearby port where more skillful medical attention could be secured.

By August 18, 1902, Mr. Morgan's log reports, in his inimitable style: "This day we are sight a large schools of large sperms whale we saw whale all day long untill night we did not lowered on account we are full ship it is to bad we are not 200 tons biggest. . . ."

On August 22 another member of the ship's company was lost when John Perry, a boatsteerer, died. Of what cause, Mr. Morgan does not say and his entries in the log simply record the facts:

Friday, August 22, "at 5.30 John Perry pass away dead land bearing N. by E."

Saturday, August 23, "we came to bury John Perry."

Wednesday, August 27, "we sold John Perry personally effects at auction for $10. 75¢ in his purse. . . ."

They arrived at San Francisco October 28, 1902, having taken sixty whales and brought back a cargo valued at almost $33,000.

In 1902 Captain Earle returned to command and this time he was accompanied not only by his wife but by a three-year-old son, Jamie, today a retired professor of engineering living in Caldwell, New Jersey. The 1902 voyage began with a swing down to the Marquesas Islands, then up to the Bonin Islands and finished on the Japan grounds, returning to San Francisco October 27, 1903. Jamie Earle was very young and his memories of the voyage are rather sketchy, but he does recall that he rather idolized big George Christian, the second mate, who made toys for him and devoted much of his off-watch time to the lad. The playground for Jamie was the deck aft of the mainmast, for he was made to observe the rigid protocol that prevailed aboard whalers. Members of the afterguard stayed aft of the mainmast unless duty called them forward, and the foremast hands did not come aft unless ordered to do so. On pleasant days Mrs. Earle would take the boy up on the roof of the hurricane house to have a clearer view of the horizon. At night he slept in a swinging hammock or box bed which hung from the overhead beams of the day cabin. He had tried

Captain James A. M. Earle, his wife Honor and son Jamie (James W.).

James W. (Jamie) Earle, in a toy boat on the deck of the *Morgan* about 1903. The boat was made for him by George Christian, then second mate. Courtesy J. W. Earle.

The Earles before their marriage: he as a young man in Honolulu, and she in Auckland, New Zealand. Courtesy Mr. and Mrs. John McNatt.

sleeping on the transom up behind the built-in sofa but with the ship rolling or pitching at all he could not stay on a mattress.

On the next voyage Captain Earle sailed with the *Morgan* on November 18, 1903, and after a sortie toward Guam went up to the Japan grounds to finish the cruise. The ship returned to San Francisco in October, 1904, with a good catch and Captain Earle left to cross the country again by rail. This was the last trip of the *Morgan* out of San Francisco, for when she sailed again a month later she was headed for her home port of New Bedford.

The whaling grounds in the northern Pacific were far from being "fished out," but with the price of whale oil and bone dropping, the short Pacific voyages were no longer as profitable as they once had been. Fitting out expenses were higher and with the "crimps" and sailors' boarding house masters in complete control of the waterfront, it became increasingly expensive to hire a crew. On his last voyage in the *Morgan* from San Francisco, Captain Earle had to pay well over $1,200 "blood money" to the crimps to get a crew. It was at about this time that most of the New Bedford fleet straggled home after a long stay in the Pacific and the *Morgan* was one of them.

At a San Francisco wharf. Note black whaleboats. Courtesy San Francisco Maritime Museum, Roy D. Graves Collection.

CHAPTER VII

The Troubled Voyage Home

CAPTAIN EDWIN J. REED was the new master of the *Charles W. Morgan* when she sailed through the Golden Gate for the last time on November 25, 1904, headed for New Bedford by way of the South Seas after an absence of some eighteen years.

The old crew which had been with Captain Earle on the previous voyage had been paid off and an entire new gang was in the forecastle. That they were a bad lot was evident from the first and trouble began before the bark was a month out. Because of abuses in the past, seamen's rights were being strongly asserted by the turn of the century and crew trouble of a different sort began to plague shipmasters and owners. "Sea lawyers" were found more frequently in forecastles and court cases became more common. These sea lawyers were seamen who had acquired some knowledge and understanding of the laws designed to protect the rights of seamen and were almost invariably natural born troublemakers. They loved to stir up dissatisfaction and turmoil, but were sure to keep well in the background when it started.

There is some indication that Captain Reed was aware of difficulties to come, for he took the precaution of preparing a second log in a form prescribed by the government in which only entries relating to the conduct of the crew were made. All entries in the log were signed by both the master and the mate, Emanuel Morgan, the only man to stay over in the ship from the previous voyage.

The mate heard of a plan set forth by a seaman named Charles King to embark on a program of disobedience to orders in an effort to goad the officers into using force, in which case they could be sued when the ship arrived in port. King apparently tried this tactic when the vessel was only a short time at sea and was put in irons until he agreed to better behavior. The next entry in the log followed the refusal of Juan Alvis and Lewis Almeda to obey a command by the chief officer, the reason given being that they were off watch. They were promptly clapped in irons until they requested release, promising to obey all commands in the future.

Incidents of this sort became common, and lying off Norfolk Island in May, 1905, seamen King, Rose, Rodman and Larcom deserted, but were recaptured and brought aboard. There they refused duty and were put in irons for several days until they promised better conduct. Rose was unrepentant, however, and in June was logged for defying the mate, who grabbed him by the collar and shook him up. The captain was very specific in noting that the mate did not strike him.

Adolf Koch, the carpenter, flatly refused to repair a pump when ordered to do so by the mate and a few days later attempted to attack the mate with an axe. He was disarmed and restrained. Another man, Manuel Rosa, was ironed after a deliberate refusal of the mate's order to go aloft.

After such trouble, Captain Reed put into Tahiti in August to lay his problems before the American consul, W. F. Daly. Daly, after investigation, had Adolf Koch and Harry Rose confined in jail to be released after the vessel sailed. Several other men deserted, but were brought back aboard and things quieted down for a time.

King, the original troublemaker, had a run-in with the mate in January, 1906, after refusing to turn out when his watch was called and using foul and abusive language toward his superior. He was clapped in double irons and was not released for two days. In May, he, with nine other men, refused to man the boats for a whale, changing their minds only when Captain Reed threatened to iron them all for the rest of the voyage.

The last incident apparently was effective and comparatively little trouble ensued thereafter. They were nearing the end of the voyage and, with a fairly good catch under hatches, Reed would have had little compunction in ironing anyone for the balance of the passage. With all the various difficulties taking place, he had still managed to take in a cargo of oil and bone valued at more than $25,000. They had been almost two years out and the cargo was not large for the period of time, but the wonder is that he was able to achieve that much.

Arriving at New Bedford in June, 1906, the *Morgan* was promptly unloaded and preparations were made to fit her out for the next voyage, which was to take her down the South Atlantic and around the Cape of Good Hope to the Indian Ocean. Once again the Wings called on Captain Earle to command her. After overseeing most of the fitting out, he was joined by Mrs. Earle and on August 11, 1906, the *Morgan* towed to sea. One of the hands in the forecastle was the Manuel Rosa who had made the previous voyage from San Francisco, and he was soon embroiled with the third mate. A fist fight resulted, leaving the mate with a bad cut and other injuries which forced him to lay up for several days. Captain Earle, always a strict disciplinarian, clapped Rosa in irons for a week and the man deserted early the next year at Port Natal.

It was not the hands who gave Earle the most trouble, however, but the first mate, Judson James, the other mates and several of the boatsteerers, with the exception of George Christian, who was still second mate. James was critical of all the captain's actions and it is obvious that trouble was brewing from the first. Of the original crew, less than a third of them were recorded as good men in the Wing account books. It is small wonder that James Earle began to regret having taken the ship out and early in 1907 he apparently began to think seriously of resigning the command. He had done quite well whaling in the vicinity of the Crozets in the south Indian Ocean, and in April, 1907, he put into Port Natal to unload oil and bone for shipping home by steamship. He also fired the first and third mates and three other boatheaders as well as several of the crew. Other crew members in addition to Rose deserted and it was necessary to sign on local men as replacements.

Apparently this succession of events caused Captain Earle to arrive at a final decision to resign and he wired J. & W. R. Wing to send out a replacement skipper if one could be found.

According to the Wing records, Captain Hiram Nye took over the command at Durban about July 19, 1907, and Captain and Mrs. Earle came home by steamer. His health was not of the best and he was apparently glad to consider retirement. He did make at least one more whaling voyage as master of the bark *Alice Knowles* but then retired ashore permanently. A younger son, Norman Earle, accompanied his father and mother on the last voyage.

Captain Nye carried on with the *Morgan*, working up to the Mozambique Channel and back down to the Crozets before heading the ship homeward in the leisurely passage up the South Atlantic by way of the Cape Verde Islands and the Azores. More men had deserted or been discharged, and when the vessel finally arrived at New Bedford in July, 1908, only nine or ten of the original crew were with her.

CHAPTER VIII

The Second Broken Voyage

C APTAIN ARTHUR O. GIBBONS was appointed as next master of the bark and he took her out September 2, 1908, on what was to be another broken voyage. The crew, according to the Wing Company records, appears to have been a good one on the whole. There was very little trouble and the voyage went as smoothly as could be expected at that time. The records indicate some sickness aboard and the cooper-carpenter and engineer-blacksmith both died at Durban in May, 1909. Several of the hands turned out to be poor at their job but generally the crew performed well.

Captain Gibbons was stricken by illness while at Durban and apparently wired the owners for a replacement. In the meantime, records indicate that the *Morgan* sailed in charge of Joseph Roderick, the first mate, who was a good whaleman but no navigator. To act in that capacity, a William Haggie was signed on. Captain Gibbons's health did not improve and Captain Charles S. Church, formerly in the bark *Andrew Hicks,* took command. He was accompanied by his wife, who was signed on as assistant navigator. Mrs. Church, the former Charlotte Ott, was the daughter of a San Francisco pilot and had made the voyage around Cape Horn with her husband when he brought the *Andrew Hicks* back to New Bedford from the West Coast. She did assist her husband in navigation and also kept the log when in the

Captain Charles W. Church and his wife Charlotte, who made two quite successful voyages on the *Morgan* in 1913. Mrs. Church, the former Charlotte Ott, daughter of a San Francisco bay pilot, acted as assistant navigator and logkeeper. Courtesy Mrs. Marian F. Church.

Morgan. Her entries were very meticulous, noting latitude, longitude, course, distance, variation, barometer, thermometer, wind force, sea and weather. She also made a regular practice of setting bottles adrift with notes in them giving the name of the vessel, position and weather condition at the time.

Flashes of humor enlightened the routine recording and Mrs. Church showed a feminine interest in other than strict ship routine. One of the first entries she made in the *Morgan's* log was to record the death of Major, a pet cat who had apparently outlived his time. Later, the steerage cat gave birth to a solitary kitten which she described as "an addition to the ship's crew." On June 25, 1910, she wrote, "killed fourteen scrawny chickens tonight. The whole lot won't make a good dinner." In August there is a dryly humorous note: "We have two live pigs, one rooster, four cats and almost twenty canary bird — no fear of starving for a while." She herself suffered from asthma and was very conscious of those members of the crew who were ill, several having been forced to lay up from time to time.

Apparently the mate, Joseph Roderick, had left the ship when Captain Church arrived and a man named J. J. Senna was hired to replace him. Strange actions on Senna's part caused the captain to investigate more thoroughly and it was found that he was insane. He therefore did not go to sea with the vessel. Nicholas Francis, the third mate, was promoted and came home eventually as mate. The voyage ended at New Bedford in September, 1910, the return on the cargo being somewhat higher than that of the previous voyage.

After a long winter layover while refitting, the *Morgan* sailed on May 10, 1911, once more under command of Captain Church, accompanied by Lottie, again signed on as assistant navigator. On this trip she did not keep the log, the task being assigned to William H. Griffiths, the mate. George Christian was still aboard as second mate with Thomas Stokes and Shadrach Tilton as third and fourth mates respectively. The crew were an indifferent lot and many of them deserted at Fayal. In fact, at one time, only three men of the original crew were aboard. Some returned and others were shipped to take the place of those who did not. Isaac Joab, the original cook, was taken seriously ill when less than three months out of New Bedford and died on September 5, 1911. Griffiths's log records: "At 8 a.m. called all hands Mr. Christian read him a funeral sermon and he was buried from the starboard gangway with all respect of our crew."

The *Morgan* finished out the year cruising down the South Atlantic, then doubled the Cape of Good Hope. By April 13, 1912, she put into Port Natal, where the crew painted her rigging and did other work on her. On April 17 the mate notes that all ships in the harbor were flying their ensigns at half mast out of respect to those lost in the *Titanic.* Three men deserted but returned by sailing day and two men were punished for fighting, although in what way is not stated.

In October, 1912, they were at Durban where the project of re-tubing the donkey boiler was undertaken. Apparently this had never been done since the boiler and engine had been installed in preparation for the 1886 voyage. The job took some time and it was late in November before the vessel was ready to sail. No crew trouble was reported in the interim, although an unexplainable entry appears in the log which states that on Sunday, November 5, Manuel Claudino went ashore and "was arrested for being *sober!*" Since Claudino is listed in the Wing records as a "good boatsteerer and a reliable man," it could only have been the mate's sense of humor which prompted the note.

On March 29, 1913 they took a sperm whale and when cutting in the next day found more than fifteen pounds of ambergris, which at the time was worth several hundred dollars a pound.

In May, 1913 the *Morgan* put in at St. Helena, where several men were shipped to take the place of deserters. Among them was a man listed in the log as Frederick Young, who was mentally disturbed. He began acting very strangely and one day climbed down over the bow to the bobchains and refused to come aboard. He finally had to be dragged up by force. Some days later he went on another rampage and the captain had him put in irons in the 'tween decks for a time. He caused no one any harm, but the rest of the crew heaved a sigh of relief when he paid off at New Bedford. The voyage ended at New

Crew setting sail at main pinrail.

Bedford August 9, 1913, and although the price of sperm oil had dropped from 63 cents to 48 cents per gallon since the previous voyage, the ship grossed over $44,000. Even though the voyage had been profitable the owners decided to lay the ship up. She was stripped and towed to Fairhaven across the harbor where she remained for the next three years.

Captain Benjamin D. Cleveland in day cabin.

CHAPTER IX

The Wings Sell Out

FOR a time it appeared that the *Morgan*'s whaling days were over. Lying neglected and forlorn at a Fairhaven wharf she seemed to have come to the end of her seventy-five-year career at last. Her paint grew shabbier every day, while shore dust and dirt settled in the nooks and crannies around her deck. The ironwork rusted and what rigging there was left became Irish pennants waving listlessly in the breeze or ragged strands of wire where the serving and parcelling rotted away.

Fortunately, Captain Benjamin Cleveland, looking for a vessel in which to make a voyage after sperm and sea elephant oil to Desolation Island in the far southern ocean, knew vessels well enough to realize that the old bark was not yet beyond redemption. After going over her carefully, he approached the Wing Company with a view toward buying her. With backing from several other investors, he arranged to purchase all but 4/64 which were held by the estate of William R. Wing. The price paid was only about $6,000 and Captain Cleveland retained 24/64, enough to assure him of control. Fitting out expenses were heavy, however, even though nothing was done that was not absolutely necessary. A few rotted spots in hood ends and butts of planking were filled with troweling cement and much of the sails and gear were leftovers from her former voyages or purchased secondhand.

The *Charles W. Morgan* laid up at Union Wharf, Fairhaven, at the end of her Whaling career. Courtesy Kendall Whaling Museum.

A small windfall in the form of a semicharter by a motion picture company paid some of the bills. The company was making a film called *Miss Petticoats,* starring Alice Brady, one of the foremost luminaries of the silent era, and since some of the scenes were laid aboard a whaling ship, they were as delighted to find the *Charles W. Morgan* available as Captain Cleveland was to welcome them aboard. No alterations were made to the hull except to nail a new name — *Harpoon* — over the old one and since the company also assumed some of the fitting out expense as well as paying a leasing or chartering fee, the old skipper was more than pleased.

The film was completed during the summer and after a final session on the railway to check the bottom, refasten the copper where necessary and thoroughly clean it, the *Morgan* was ready to sail. This

Charles W. Morgan hauled out on the ways at Fairhaven about 1916. Courtesy Kendall Whaling Museum.

she did in September, 1916, with Captain Cleveland in command and a crew of some thirty-one men, most of them experienced Portuguese-American whalemen. The first and second mates were John D. Lopes and John Louber, with Walter Thompson as third officer. Boatsteerers were Charles Johnson, Edward Baures, Antone Fonseca and Benjamin W. Cleveland, probably a son or nephew of the master. The steward was Edward Jan and the carpenter, Edward M. Morse.

They sighted the first whale of the voyage on September 20, but although they lowered three boats none was able to get close enough to dart an iron and they had to return to the ship with nothing to show for their pains. Two days later they sighted a school, or pod, of whales and again the three boats were lowered. This time the bow boat killed their whale, but the waist boat was stove and lost their whale, while the larboard boat struck but the iron was drawn and they also lost theirs.

Twice more they struck and killed whales before they sighted the island of St. Vincent in the Cape Verdes on November 9. After lying over for a couple of days, they sailed across to Brava and lay there for two more days making some minor repairs. Working down south, they finally sighted Desolation Island on February 11, 1917, but were some ten days beating up to it against head winds. There they anchored and began their hunt for sea elephants. Similar to seals but larger, their blubber is rich with oil.

Hunting went on in routine fashion until April 19 when a simple entry in the log told a tragic story. In Captain Cleveland's very original spelling, it reads:

> About 10 o'clock a.m. very moderat whether but the see was very bad Boats went on shoor to bring of eliphant bluber and the surf riased up and turned one boat over and lost 4 men Ther names Richards Moor Aguste Lemas Albert Rubeiro and Daniel O'conor The rest of the crew on duty at Desolation Island.
>
> Signed: Benjamin D. Cleveland master
> John D. Lopes cheffe mate
> Charles Johnson boatsteerer

No other details are given in the log which, like most other documents of its type, records only the unadorned facts.

Leaving Desolation Island on May 12, the *Morgan* worked northward into the South Atlantic and on August 8 raised the island of St. Helena, where she anchored next day. There she lay for eight days while fresh water was taken aboard, some repairs made and the crew given a chance to stretch their legs ashore, a watch at a time. Sailing again August 16, the vessel followed a course to the West Indies and on September 23 she anchored at the island of Dominica, and next day sailed for St. Eustacia. Apparently Captain Cleveland, with a war on, decided to make his way northward by "island hopping." They sighted several sailing vessels and steamers as they worked their way toward home but nothing eventful occurred. (Captain Cleveland is elsewhere reported to have told people in New Bedford that they narrowly missed colliding with a mine outside of Dominica but nowhere in the log is there mention of any such incident.)

Later the bark reached St. Bartholomew, but shortly thereafter

Charles W. Morgan lying in at New Bedford in company of bark Wanderer. A. F. Packard photograph.

the log ends abruptly and no details of the passage up the American coast are recorded. She arrived home October 23, 1917, with a cargo valued at $21,000.

With the United States fully involved in the war, Captain Cleveland decided to sell out while he had a chance. His shares went to Captain John A. Cook of Provincetown, a veteran whaleman and shipowner. Since Captain Cook was a resident of Provincetown, he documented the *Morgan* there and for the first time in her long career the vessel showed a hailing port other than New Bedford on her stern. She continued to fit out at the old port, however, and when she sailed on her next voyage in July, 1918, she took her departure as she had always done.

Captain Joseph F. Edwards was the master for the voyage. A native of the island of Flores in the Azores, he was a younger brother of

75

Captain Antone Edwards, who had been master of American whalers for several years. Joseph Edwards had been whaling in numerous vessels, starting as cabin boy and finally, with his new master's license in his pocket, he took command of the *Charles W. Morgan.*

Risking interception by German submarines or commerce raiders, Captain Edwards took his vessel down through the West Indies to the Brazil banks off the South American coast. There he was moderately successful in killing whales and when the *Morgan* returned to New Bedford on September 7, 1919, it was found that her 1,150-barrel cargo was worth over $25,000. This inspired Captain Edwards to get back to sea as soon as possible and slightly over a month later the *Morgan* was heading across the Atlantic toward the Cape Verdes where the captain hoped to recruit more men. They did not make the islands, however, and turned back toward the South Atlantic. There, some seven months out, Captain Edwards became seriously ill and was confined to his berth. His condition became such that the mate, alarmed and recognizing the need for skilled medical attention, decided to take the vessel home, although they had only 750 barrels of oil aboard. She arrived at New Bedford July 16, 1920. With the war over and the price of oil dropping, her 750 barrels brought less than $9,000.

Since Captain Edwards had not fully recovered, Captain John Gonsalves was appointed to take the *Morgan* out on what was to be her final whaling voyage. It was beset with difficulties, including serious trouble with the crew, several of whom were discharged at Dominica. To replace them, a motley collection of local men, including tailor's apprentices, clerks and sundry other inexperienced individuals only anxious to get to the United States, were signed on. Whaling went on, however, and on May 28, 1921, the *Morgan* came home to discharge a 2,702-barrel cargo. Had the wartime price of 73 cents a gallon still prevailed, the vessel would have had a fine voyage financially, but the price was down to 30 cents a gallon and the total value of the cargo was $25,533.90.

CHAPTER X

The End of Whaling

WITH the time approaching when the vessel would need a very complete refit, the future did not look bright for further whaling. While the owners were considering the future, an opportunity to return to film making saved the *Morgan* from obscurity. Elmer Clifton, formerly of the D. W. Griffith studio, was directing a film to be called *Down to the Sea in Ships,* starring Raymond McKee and Marguerite Courtot and featuring, among others, Clara Bow, later to be famed as the "It" girl.

For the making of this film the *Morgan* returned to the rig of her earliest days — that of a full-rigged ship, although not correctly in all details. Oddly enough, the sailing scenes were taken of the bark *Wanderer* and the actual whaling scenes from the schooner *Gaspe* on the West Indian grounds. Hardly had the one film been completed when Paramount decided to make Joseph Hergesheimer's novel *Java Head.* The *Morgan* was sailed up to Salem, Massachusetts, where she took the part of an East India merchantman, although to the initiated she looked like nothing but the whaler she was. Starring in *Java Head* were Leatrice Joy, Jacquelin Logan, Raymond Hatton, George Fawcett and other top stars of the day.

Her whaling days over and any future film career unlikely, the bark was laid up again. She was not entirely forgotten, however, for

The *Charles W. Morgan* at a (new Bedford) wharf as fitted out for making of movie *Java Head* in 1924. Captain James Tilton in foreground. Courtesy H. H. Kynett.

Harry Neyland, a well-known New Bedford marine artist, was doing his utmost to arouse sufficient interest among municipal and state authorities to take over the ship as a museum. He personally acquired many of her shares and in 1924 was listed as master and managing owner holding a 27/32 interest.

The problem was almost solved once and for all when the steamer *Sankaty* caught fire at her New Bedford wharf and drifted across the harbor when her lines burned through. The *Morgan* was lying at a Fairhaven wharf and the blazing steamer came to rest against her port quarter. Fortunately the Fairhaven fire department was able to prevent a general conflagration and the *Morgan* was undamaged beyond an area of scorched paint in hull and superstructure.

Despite this close call the New Bedford city authorities failed to take any action nor could the Massachusetts legislature be interested. Organizations were formed to raise money and at one time an early

Burned-out hull of the steamer *Sankaty* resting alongside the *Charles W. Morgan* at Fairhaven, July 1924.

The *Charles W. Morgan* as she appeared at Colonel Green's estate following death of the financier. Whaling Enshrined photograph.

The *Charles W. Morgan* comes up the Mystic River to the Seaport on November 8, 1941.

effort was made to have the *Morgan* declared a national shrine. Nothing was successful, however, until Neyland had the inspiration to get in touch with Colonel Edward H. R. Green, the wealthy grandson of Edward "Black Hawk" Robinson, principal owner of the ship from 1849 to 1859. Green, a man of many interests and sudden enthusiasms, seems to have needed little persuading and soon had a permanent berth prepared for her, surrounded by coffer dams, at his South Dartmouth summer estate. The ship was completely refitted, sails were made and bent, and a regular crew of whalemen hired to stand by under the direction of Captain George Fred Tilton, a renowned Martha's Vineyard whaling master. The ship was opened to the public and became a mecca for thousands of people interested in whaling and maritime history in general. Unfortunately, in the last years of his life Colonel Green seemed to lose interest, and following his death in 1935 it was learned that he had left no money whatsoever for the continued maintenance of the old ship.

Harry Neyland and others tried their best to raise funds to keep the ship intact as she was, but it was not long after the depression, and money raising was more difficult than ever. Without constant attention the *Morgan* began to deteriorate again and when the 1938 hurricane struck she almost broke up. She was still stout enough to withstand the fury of the elements, however, and although washed partly out of her bed and sustaining other superficial damage, she did survive.

Carl Cutler, one of the founders of The Marine Historical Association and curator at Mystic Seaport, then entered into negotiation with the owners of the *Charles W. Morgan*. The owners at that time were a group of men formed into a corporation known as Whaling Enshrined. Cutler assured them that he had a definite promise of financial support to repair and maintain the vessel if she could be brought to Mystic Seaport. Much as the owners and many New Bedford people hated to see her leave, they finally realized that the necessary funds could not be raised there, and rather than see her disintegrate, they agreed to let her go to Mystic.

Removal from the berth at South Dartmouth and temporary re-

Drying sails at New Bedford. Courtesy Kendall Whaling Museum.

pairs to enable her to be towed to Mystic were expensive and time-consuming, but at last, on November 8, 1941, the *Charles W. Morgan* came up the Mystic River to her new home port in tow of a Coast Guard cutter. Again her luck was holding, for had it been only a little later, after Pearl Harbor, she might never have been moved and would doubtless have become a wreck before the end of the war. Although Carl Cutler and his small crew did their best to get materials for rebuilding, she suffered further deterioration before the war came to an end and it was possible to undertake major repairs once more.

Gradually, a rebuilding project forged ahead. Many new spars were installed and by 1960 all her topside planking had been renewed above the waterline. Unfortunately, it was almost impossible to secure well-seasoned lumber and it soon became evident that much of the work was not holding up well. Unless a major job was undertaken, the ship would be doomed in a few more years. It was imperative she be saved since she had been declared a National Historic Landmark by order of the Secretary of the Interior in 1967.

Expert consultants were engaged and investigations of every kind undertaken to get an idea of her real condition. Test borings were made through planks, timber and frames, and stability calculations were made. It has finally been decided that a complete and careful rebuilding and refitting is necessary and the project is now under way.

She will not have the questionable ship rig which is familiar to so many, but will return to the guise in which she did most of her whaling. Her hull will be black with simple white stripes at main rail and plank sheer and her rig will be that of a double topsail bark. The reason for this lies in the fact that her earliest appearance of hull and rig cannot be factually documented, whereas her appearance during the longest segment of her whaling career is familiar. Under this rig she worked from 1867 to 1921.

Through the generosity of the late Henry S. duPont, funds were provided which are being used to complete the working shipyard and lift dock where the *Morgan* can be hauled and repaired. She will be taken out of her present sand and gravel base and thereafter will be kept afloat in her natural element. The experience of the past years in

Traveling wheel, known to most seamen as shincracker or toejammer. Note compass in after end of skylight.

attempting full maintenance has convinced those responsible that she will deteriorate less and be far easier to maintain if kept afloat. The shipyard facility makes this possible, not only for the *Morgan* but for all the other craft at the Seaport. Thus the *Charles W. Morgan* will enter upon the last phase of her career, to be preserved as a true memorial of the great days of the whaling industry, seamen and ships.

Charles W. Morgan Crew Lists

Below are listed the crew members of the *Charles W. Morgan* throughout her whaling career of thirty-seven recorded voyages from September 6, 1841 through September 9, 1920. The list is complete insofar as records presently known allow. The bulk of her crew members was obtained from the records of the J. & W. R. Wing and Company account books covering her voyage from December 1, 1863 through the voyage of May 10, 1911. Where possible, the names were cross-checked among all three of the sources for this compilation: official custom house records of the vessel, where extant; New Bedford Whaling newspaper — "Whaleman's Shipping List"; and the Wing Account Books. In some cases only the crew which shipped for the initial leg of the voyage was available. Subsequent shipping, discharging and desertion records are sometimes incomplete, depending on the voyage.

This compilation is not clear cut, since names were frequently spelled in two or three ways, due to the illiteracy of many of the men. Furthermore, people would often change their names when shipping if they were going to sea to get away from home or escape the law. In the case of a conflict in spelling, the official government records were taken in preference to any other. In cases of questionable legibility, the most legible was taken, if not in conflict with official records.

There is also the matter of the same name appearing on subsequent voyages. Unfortunately, time and incomplete records did not allow for checking to be completely certain that the name applied to the same man. The long career of George P. Christian is one example which may be correct but needs further checking to substantiate fully.

The author is greatly indebted to the National Archives, and to Reginald B. Hegarty of the New Bedford Free Public Library for invaluable assistance in making records available for use in compiling this crew list.

The compilation is in two parts: a chronological listing by voyage, and an alphabetical listing of crewmen. Asterisks indicate those who completed the voyages.

CREW LISTS

VOYAGE 1 — September 6, 1841 — January 1, 1845

*Thomas A. Norton, Master
Charles S. Chadwick, 1st Mate,
   discharged at Payta
*James C. Osborn, 2nd Mate
*William A. Look, 3rd Mate

*Allen M. Athearn
Orlando Blake
Thomas K. Coffin
*William H. Coffin
*James Connelly
Thomas Curtis
Henry Dallez
*William Dunham
*Samuel O. Fisher
*Zenas Gould
William Harris
*Samuel J. Hudson
Holmes Jernegan
*Nathan M. Jernegan
*Miles A. Johnson
*Manuel Lopez

*John A. Luce
Barney McGee
*Stillman Manter
*Timothy Mayhew
George Morgan
Vicente Muscoso
*William R. Norton
*William Osborn
George Porter
Samuel Robinson
Charles Scriber
Isaac C. Smith
*Philander Smith
*Manuel Tavares
Jacob Thompson
*Abraham Weaver

VOYAGE 2 — June 10, 1845 — December 9, 1848

*John D. Samson, Master
*William W. Clement, 1st Mate
*Frederick Vincent, 2nd Mate
*William Griffin, 3rd Mate

*John Antone
Diego Aquisa
William Black
Robert Bolton
*Amos Brown
Henry J. Coop
Charles Cushman (died)
*John Doramus
William Firth
J. Frank
*Zenas Gould
William H. Herbert
*Enoch Hookway
William Hundray
Josiah Hutchinson

*John Lattick
Henry A. Lincoln
*Antone F. Mayo
William McLane
*William McLoughlin
George Morgan
Thomas W. Owens
*Thacher Packard
John E. Stafford
*James Tate
*Henry Tilley
William Tootha
Abraham H. Weaver
Henry White
*James D. Whiteside

VOYAGE 3 — June 5, 1849 — May 27, 1853

*John D. Samson, Master
*Thacher Packard, 1st Mate
*William Griffin, 2nd Mate
*Roland Briggs, 3rd Mate
John Adams
*William Auza
*Stephen Barnum
John Barker
*Benjamin Butman
Amasa Colby
*William L. Covell
*Charles Coy
Vincent D. Crowl
Lewis Dorr
*George Duffy

Enos Eastwood
*Moses F. Gardner
*Mathew Gilgannon
*Nelson C. Haley
Joseph Maxwell
*Benjamin Olney
James W. Parker
*Thomas Phillips
Ben Rotch
Thomas Ryan
*Daniel W. Sampson

*Thomas A. Tyler, Jr.   Francis Warner
*Smith Tucker   Martin Whitehead
 David Van Riper   *Joseph Whitman

VOYAGE 4 — September 20, 1853 — April 27, 1856

*Tristram P. Ripley, Master
 Stephen Devoll, 1st Mate,
  discharged at Lahàmor
*Ariel Norton, 2nd Mate
*Joseph C. Airey   Kaavea
*Manuel Alexander   Kaulahea
 Antone   *Antone Lewis
 David E. Bean   John Macey
 Bemamona   *Thomas Malone
 James Boyd   Joe Manuel
*William Corey   Keav Nin
 William Denzmore *Charles E. Phelps
*Alvin H. Davis   Jacinth Pray
*Samuel T. Davis   *John Read
 William F. Doyle   *John Riccols
 John Druse   *Benjamin Ripley
*John Erwin   *Justus J. Sampson
 J. P. Fisher   *Whitcomb Sampson
*Samuel H. Haines   *Frederick Snadaker
 William Hall   *John M. Tucker
 Hawamnu   Peter Williams
*Charles Jackson   *George F. Winslow

VOYAGE 5 — September 15, 1856 — April 16, 1859

*Thomas N. Fisher, Master
*Thomas W. Johnson, 1st Mate
*Samuel T. Davis, 2nd Mate
*David Carrington, 3rd Mate
*Charles W. Addams   Tom Ascension
 Eugene H. Anderson James O. Brian
 Friday Ascension   Franco Brooks
 Joe Ascension   *John Cabit

William G. Crowell
*John R. Cuff
Charles D. Daggett
*Antonio de Medeiros
Manuel Deos
William H. Drew
James H. Evans
*Henry Francis
*Peter Galena
*James Hamlin
James Harrison
*Edwin Height
*Edward Hobbs
Charles G. Kline
George M. Lam
Edward LeBaron
George McLean
*William B. Marshant

*Jose Miguel
*Joseph N. Mill
*Albert Palmer
*Edward L. Pangburn
*Michael Pease
Charles Pitts
John Raphael
*Dickenson Read
*John Reed
*Alexander Reyot
William Robinson
Joseph Roderiguez
George Ross
Smith Rowland
Antonio Sabina
*Antone Sylvia
Lewis Verra
*William Young

VOYAGE 6 — October 4, 1859 — May 12, 1863

*James A. Hamilton, Master
*George Smith, 1st Mate
*John Williams, 2nd Mate
*Peter Sylvia, 3rd Mate

Daniel Andrews
David Baker
Martin Barrett
David Beaton
Lewis Becker
Truman B. Braley
*Ansel E. Brealy
Thomas Brown
Rodney S. Campbell
Henry Carter
Joseph Carter
Charles
Henry Clay

Manuel da Rose Coello
J. J. Coleman
Charles Crim
Robert Darling
Charles Davis
Jose de Canto
Jose de la Costa
Ceracio de la Rosa
Nicholas de la Rosa
Joseph N. de Malo
Dick
John Dyer
Henry Eldridge

John Enos

George Faville

Peter Fernandez

Barney Fisher

Joseph Fisher

Nicholas Gabrino

George Gibson

George W. Gifford

Antonio Gonzales

Silvanus S. Gove

John Grady

Richard Griswold

Horace O. Hancock

Luman G. Hensted

Henry Hillman

Jarvis G. Horton

Juan N. Janos

William B. Johnson

Kaluna

Kealoha

Julian Knowles

John H. Lathrop

Thomas F. Laycock (died)

Alonzo Levally

Antone Lopez

Louis

Anton Ludwig

Francis McEvena

John McIntyre

James McTier

Richard H. Mead

John Martins

Harry Mokii

Edward Ormesby

Asa Page

John Perano

Frank Perry

Thomas Philbrook

Andrew J. Phillips

James Phillips

John Pleasant

Daniel Quinn

Elijah Rathbone

Samuel N. Richardson

Riley

William Roach

John Roche

Antone Roderick

Manuel Roderick

Bill Rotomar

Bob Rotomar

Frank Rotomar

Friday Rotomar

Jack Rotomar

Peter Rotomar

Manuel Saldinia

Thomas Sherman

William H. Shippen

Antonio Silvia

Peter Silvia

William Slater

Charles Smith

Charles Solano

Jose Tenelasco

John Thompson

Guillermo Torres

James A. Tripp

Francisco Ulloa

Alex Upham

Robert S. Valentine

James Wallace

Thomas C. Webb

William

William Whitelaw

James Wilson   John Wright
James S. Wise

Lack of original record prevents full identification of those who completed
voyage #6

VOYAGE 7 — December 1, 1863 — June 12, 1867

*Thomas C. Landers, Master
*Charles W. Chace, 1st Mate
*William Harlow, 2nd Mate
*Benjamin White, 3rd Mate

*Charles Amory   *John Jose
 William P. Anderson   *A. H. Lambert
*William F. Benton   Arthur Landers (drowned)
*Antone Christ   N. Marinda
*Daniel Connus   *Edward Parrott
*John Crowley   Felix Reno
*William Curran   James R. Royce
*Manuel Francis   Joseph Silva
*Elijah Fuller   John Smith
*John Gardner   *Bartholomew Sullivan
*Antone L. Gonsalves   *Oliver P. Tufts
*William Gorman   *James Williams

VOYAGE 8 — July 17, 1867 — August 16, 1871

*George Athearn, Master
 Alvan H. Davis, 1st Mate (died)
*Frederick C. Swain, 2nd Mate
*Frank Roderick, 3rd Mate
*Edwin W. Athearn, 4th Mate

 Antone Aenas   Albert N. Butts
 John Andrews   Joseph Carvo
*Matthais Antonio   William L. G. Chace
 Magill Agusta   *Jerome Chochin
 Joseph Barre   Santa de Croze
 Ben Besanta   *Antone M. de Suza
 August Bottzer   Antone Dolires
 Charles M. Brown   *Manuel Dundrade
 Joseph Brown   William H. Fish

Jack Fisher

Phillip Folpe

Francisco Foster

Antonio Francisco

*Anthony J. Frates

John Frates

John Grob

William Handy

Joking Michael

Oswald Julp

Jack Kanaka

Mois Kanaka

*Fred LeBaron

Antone Lewis

Enas Lewis

*Hiram W. Look

William McHenry

James C. McKeever

Jim Mangra

William Munroe

G. H. Myers

*Antone Nesmith

Thomas Nesmith

Jules Nicholas

*Maul M. Nunes

John Orrotanga

*John Silva

George Schlick

George H. Smith

John Smith

Lewis Smith

Levi Swift

Manuel Thomas

J. E. Waterbury

Ishmael White

Bob Whytootake

VOYAGE 9 — September 26, 1871 — October 31, 1874

*John M. Tinkham, Master

*Wanton S. Beauvais, 1st Mate

*Andrew Jackson, 2nd Mate

*Frank Roderick, 3rd Mate

Antone Nesmith, 4th Mate

Charles Adams

Amille Adlos

St. Cyr. Adolphe

Nemoine Anacoser

Enos Avilla

Howard Beaumont

Theodore L. Bennett (died)

William Charles

*Leonte D. Cross

Alcide Dart

Frank Deas

*Joseph De Lombo

*Jose de Simos

Bud. O. Fees

John Flynn

*Manuel Francis

Lewis Gonsalves

Joseph Hall

Marbois Henry

Alphonses James

Philo M. Joan

James D. Keizer

Joseph King

Merdene Kiouse

August Kornumpt
F. Lamb
Joseph Leamon
Antone M. Lemos
Mohee Lewis
*Hiram W. Look
Domingo Lopez
August Macoxa
Joe Martin
A. Meail
*Herman Meinhardt
Jacob Meinhardt
*John Miller
*Pliney Mitchell
Joseph Monzar
Thomas Morgan

Patrick O'Brien
*Manuel J. Perris
Philip Rozette
*Louis Santo
*William Schmidt
*Richard Settle
John Sharpe
Charles Sheinle
Henry Smith
*John Smith
Manuel Sonares
*Mariano J. Souares
*Antonio Vieria
John M. Vincent
*John Williams
Peter Zette

VOYAGE 10 — April 23, 1875 — May 17, 1878

*John M. Tinkham, Master
*Daniel L. Ricketson, 1st Mate
Antonio Silva, 2nd Mate
*Charles L. Willis, 3rd Mate
*Eanos D. Avilla, 4th Mate

Meguil Alvez
Jose Antone
Fernando Aveira
Epolito Bernado
*Manuel Bravo
William Brown
Francisco Cabral
Manuel Cabral
C. Wells Coggeshall
Willie F. Cook
Jose Cuemintel
Manuel da Costa
Jose da Freitas
Turibio da Lomba
Manuel da Rosa

Marcellino da Silva
Jerome DeFrates
Megil Delgardo
Francisco de Souza
Jose de Mello
Carlos de Penna (died)
Jose de Soito
Charles Dowdell
Aaron W. Drew
Julio Duarte
Edward J. Dyer
Eugene W. Fish
Martin Flood
J. J. Fonseca
Manoel Fustino

Joseph Hall
Andrew Harrison
Adolphus Hayard
*Albert N. Haskins
Frank Howell
Antonio Jacinto
John Jack
Andrew Jackson
Joseph King
John Knipe
Antonio Lego
Manuel Lopes
George T. Marshall
Jose A. Martino
Pedro Miller
Jose Monteira

Charles O. Morse
Antone Penaro
Irving A. Perry
Joseph S. Perry
*Charles M. Sanborn
Fred Schneickhardt
Joas J. Senna
Albert Silva
Joas Simoes
*John E. D. Smith
George J. Thomas
Thomas H. Turner
Dixie C. Twombly
Antone Vera
Charles A. Wood
Joseph Young

VOYAGE 11 — July 17, 1878 — May 11, 1881

*Thomas L. Ellis, Master
*John B. Tobey, 1st Mate
*Joseph King, 2nd Mate
*William I. Shackley, 3rd Mate

Sabine Alps
*Megel Antone
*Manuel Arenas
*Ferdinand Avery
*Joseph A. Bailey
*William L. Baker
Samuel Brooks
Thomas Brown
*Charles F. Coleman
Antone Corea
*Manuel Coreia
James Crow
*Manuel da Costa
Henrique de Brit
Jose D. de Lemos

Rufus de Ramos
*Manuel de Roza
Jose de Silvia
John Eanos
*Arthur C. Eldridge
John Ellis
Antone Fillis
*William C. Fish
*Joseph L. Fortes
Casimere Gonsalves
*Nicholas Gonsalves
*Manuel Gracia
*John Harding
*Albert N. Haskins
*Manuel Jackson

*Oren B. Jeffers
*Peter Johnson
William Johnson
Antone Lopez
*Charles S. Manchester
Jose Marks
*Joseph Mendoze
Manuel Mitchell
Bernardo Prariea
*Antonio Rezende
*Charles Sanborn

Antone Santa
*John E. D. Smith
Jones Smith
*Joseph Sylva
Isaac Sylvia
Joseph S. Sylvia
Manuel Sylvia
Albert Thomas
*Joseph Thomas
*William W. White
*Rudolphus L. Wordell

VOYAGE 12 — July 13, 1881 — June 17, 1886

*Charles F. Keith, Master
*James F. Lawrence, 1st Mate
*Joseph King, 2nd Mate
*Peter John, 3rd Mate
James S. Howland, 4th Mate
   (drowned)
George Allibaw
Frank Alpheus
*Henry J. Clarke
*Jose Correa
Lawrence Correa
Robert W. Craig
*Manuel P. Delgado
*Goddance de Pena
Phileme de Silvia
Antone Edwards
Charles Fisher
*Henry Gelkes
Jose A. Gomez
*Casimere Gonsalves
*George Groth
John Harding
*George Hassell
*Augustus E. Hawkes

Max Herman
*William B. Keith
Antone Lopez
Jose Lopez
*Douglass McDonald
*N. A. Martin
*Jose Morano
Marcellino Morea
William H. Morey
Ernest Mountain
Jose Ramos
Earl C. Russell (died)
*Ernest Secara
Enos Seckava
*Lewis V. Semedo
Frederick Seymore
*John A. Simmons
*John E. D. Smith

James Wallace
John Wallis
*Thomas Waters

Harry Wilson
George E. Yale

VOYAGE 13 — October 6, 1886 — November 4, 1887

*George A. Smith, Master
*John S. Layton, 1st Mate
*William F. Allen, 2nd Mate
*Andrew T. Nash, 3rd Mate
*Ensign E. Baker, 4th Mate
*John Allen
*Lewis G. Andrews
*James Antone
*Edward Arnold
Joseph Bemont
*Joseph F. Branch
*Charles Brines
*George Brown
George Cody
*Crispolo de Aris
*Antonio F. de Grass
Joze de Los Santos
*Manuel P. Delgado
*John Frara
*William J. George
Bartholomew F. Gomez
Harry Hermann

G. Hirrera
*Henry W. Howland
*Orlando M. Lumbert
*Joseph Lewis
*Clement Lopez
John F. Lopez
*Willie McCormick
*William McKutchesson
*Honorio A. Martin
William J. Mitchell
Juan Quitagua
*Thomas Pena
Fred W. Robinson
*Marcellino Rose
*Otto Schuler
Joze Sequina
*John E. D. Smith

VOYAGE 14 — December 3, 1887 — November 5, 1888

*George A. Smith, Master
*Silvanus C. Waldron, 1st Mate
*John H. Gifford, 2nd Mate
*Henry Rodrigues, 3rd Mate
*Honorio A. Martin, 4th Mate
*John Andrus
Jim Antone (drowned)

*Jose Antonio
*George Brown

*Leander G. Cobb
*Dominico de Costa
*Manuel de la Rosa
 Joe Dollie
*August Engstrom
*Ben Fauste
*William J. George
*William M. Hutchinson
*Antone Joseph
 James Kennett
*Jim Kanaka
*C. Kurz
*Jacob Lena
*Manuel F. D. Limas
*John McBride
*Edward Maillot

*James Marshall
*Frank Mitchell
*Manuel Morgan
*Phillip Montes
 George Pender
 S. R. Pickersgill (drowned)
*Pat Powers
 F. H. Roberts
*Joe Santos
 Edward Sinclair
*Joe Sirvance
*Charles Stanton
 W. W. Whitney
 George Williams (died)
*Edward J. Wilson

VOYAGE 15 — November 26, 1888 — October 27, 1889

*John S. Layton, Master
*Andrew D. West, 1st Mate
*A. Spiering, 2nd Mate
*Antone Cabral, 3rd Mate
*Honorio A. Martin, 4th Mate

 Charles Alberts
*Carl Baptista
 John Ball
*George Brown
*G. W. Canover
 James Cole
*John M. Cornell, Jr.
 Charles Edwards
*Manuel F. de Limaz
 Ben Fausta
*Emidio Fernandes
*John Frazer
*W. H. Freeman
*William J. George

 Dick Kanaka
 Hallick Kanaka
 Harry Kanaka
 Pray Kanaka
*Jack Kelley
*Henry M. King
 Fred Lucas
*William McCourchison
*Edward Maillot
*James Marshall
 Antone Merry
*William J. Morris
 Teopsin Oporgydobe
 Partell

*George H. Peckham

*Stephen Pena

*John Perry

Pat Powers

*John Sablan

*Joe Santos

*Charles Smith

Chalmers Smyth

*Charles Stanton

*Jose Taitano

*George W. Topping

*Edmund Verbracken

*Joseph Vincent

VOYAGE 16 — December 5, 1889 — November 8, 1890

*John S. Layton, Master

*William F. Allen, 1st Mate

Honorio A. Martin, 2nd Mate

*Antone Cabral, 3rd Mate

*Simeon C. Leach, 4th Mate

*Adoniram J. Jones, 5th Mate

*John Branscombe

*Fred Brown

*George Brown

*Ben Castro

J. B. Cook

*John M. Cornell, Jr.

Emideo Fernandez

*Theodore Florence

William H. Griffith

B. F. Hargrave

*Otto Hartman

Jacob Jones

*Jack Kelley

Harry A. Kluge

*Joaquim Lopes

William Madigan

*Edward Maillot

*William J. Morris

*A. Nyberg

*Henry Orchatz

John Peters

*Ignacious Sablan

John Saipan

Antone Santos

Felice Selihan

*Joe Sequin

Antone Silva

*Charles Smith

*John E. Smith

*William Smith

*Charles Stanton

Tom Stephensen

G. W. Taylor

*Edmund Verbracken

Domingo Blas
Enos Chaco

Harry Bram, shipping master, reports that these two men signed for the bark *Cape Horn Pigeon* but went by mistake on *Charles W. Morgan*. As a result, neither man was paid his advance of $50 since it was not known that they were aboard.

VOYAGE 17 — December 2, 1890 — October 31, 1891

*James A. M. Earle, Master
*Daniel W. Gifford, 1st Mate
*William W. James, 2nd Mate
*Simeon Leach, 3rd Mate
*Jose de Gloria, 4th Mate

*Frank Bauer
Domingo Blas
*John Branscombe
H. D. Bowman
*George Brown
*Ben Castro
Enos Chaco (died)
*Enos de la Crus
Ignacia de la Cruz
J. De La Cruze
Vicente de la Cruze
Jose de San Nicolas
John Driver
Bernabe Enecenio
*Robert N. Flanders
Vicenti Guantanilla
*Charles S. Hait
*August Heinemann
*Edward Johnson
*Peter Johnson
Eugene Lee
*William Madigan
Charles Marston

*Felix Martinez
Nicholas Matigan
*N. Matsutara
Charles Meyers
Peter Peres
*Charles Peterson
*Ysidorio Ramos
*Celo Regis
*John Roberts
*Joseph Rodgers
*Manuel Rose
*Vicento Rose
*John S. Ross
*Felix Sablan
*Joseph Sablan
Peter Salinas
Jose Santos
*Joe Sequinda
*Hermann Smith
*John E. D. Smith
Charles Stanton
Joaquim Uuinatta
*Nelson Wilson

VOYAGE 18 — November 24, 1891 — November 7, 1892

*James A. M. Earle, Master
Robert N. Flanders, 1st Mate
*William W. James, 2nd Mate
*Frank Enos, 3rd Mate
*Charles A. Howland, 4th Mate
*Frank Bauer, 5th Mate

Tilge Aflague
*Peder Andersen
*Carl Baptista
*Jose Benchimol
*Domingo Blas
*John Branscombe
*George Brown
*Lucas Castro
*Leander G. Cobb
*Jose de Castro
*Saberin Diaz
*E. Doneburgh
Antone Gorman
*Thomas James
*Joaquim Kanaka
*Jack Kelley
*Harry A. Kluge
*Charles F. Koch

*Ben Longrero
*Felix Martines
*Ramon Mesa
*Andrew Meyer
*Nicholas Miolio
*Peter Peres
Ysidorio Ramos
Fred Richter
*Ben Rose
*John S. Ross
*Joseph Sablan
*Joe Silva
*Seraphin Silva
John Stephens
*W. H. Summers
*Venororo
James H. Walker
*Charles Winters

VOYAGE 19 — December 8, 1892 — November 9, 1893

*James A. M. Earle, Master
*Horace F. Tower, 1st Mate
*Frank Enos, 2nd Mate
*George H. Peckham, 3rd Mate

*Felix Aflague
*Peder Andersen
*Carl Baptista
*Frank Bauer
*John Branscombe
*George Brown
*Otto Carl
*Richard Carter
*Lucas Castro
*Jose de Castro
Manuel de la Conception
Juan de la Cruze
Nicholas de Salas

*Peter Feeney
Anselino Glacioas
*William A. Goering
*Antone Gomes
*John Gomes
Louis Gumatastas
*Thomas James
*William W. James
*John Jacobs
Henry Johnson
*Sam Kahaunaele
*William Kailiuli
*Joaquim Kanaka

*Jack Kelley
*Harry A. Kluge
*Charles F. Koch
*Vicento Longrero
*Peter Lopez
*John Lin
*William McDonald
*Samuel McIntyre
*Joe Manalisea
*Nicholas Miolio
*Jose Nego

*Charles Petroesch
*George Phillips
*Jose Qenehimol
*Manuel Rice
*John S. Ross
 Felix Sablan
*Seraphin Silva
 Jose Sauza
*W. H. Summers
*Charles Winters
*William H. Young

VOYAGE 20 — December 6, 1893 — November 5, 1895

*James A. M. Earle, Master
 Frederick C. Swain, 1st Mate,
    killed at sea (whale)
*William W. James, 2nd Mate
*George H. Peckham, 3rd Mate
*Joseph Avellar, 4th Mate

*Peder Andersen
 Inez Avejay
*Carl Baptista
 Thomas Barry
 Christ Berentsem
 L. Bloss
*John Branscombe
 Robert Brown
*George Brown
 B. Castro
 George P. Christian
 Auckland Cook
*Leonte de Cross
 A. de la Cruz
 J. de la Cruz
*Luis Gamatautau
 I. Guerrero
 Robert Hampton

 William Hanson
*John Jacobs
*W. Kahulio
 Joaquim Kanaka
*Jack Kelley
 Harry A. Kluge
*Charles F. Koch
 A. LaCoste
 Frank Lopes
 J. Luhan
 Phillip Mann
*Frank Mathews
 Henry Meiggs
 J. Mendolo
 Fidel Momis
 Jose Nego
 Frank A. Perry
 A. Quinn

Albert Quintal
H. Quintal
Walter H. Quintal
Carl V. Ross
J. Ross
Manuel Ross
T. Ryan
John Sablan (died at sea)
J. Santos
Manuel Santos
Mariano Santos

Joe Senner
Joe Siloa
Joe Silva
*John Silvia
T. Snell
Charles Spencer
*W. H. Summers
Hugh N. Thyrd
Joseph Vieira
Frank White
Albert Zander

VOYAGE 21 — December 2, 1895 — November 1, 1896

*James A. M. Earle, Master
*George P. Christian, 1st Mate
*Antonio Margarido, 2nd Mate
*Joe Avellar, 3rd Mate
*Julius B. Perry, 4th Mate

Nicholas Aflague
*Peder Andersen
Carl Baptista
Henry Bemis
Louis Blass
*George Brown
*Edward Carter
Jose Comanche
*Leonte de Cross
*Antonio de la Cruz
Rosario de la Rosario
*Henry Gomes
Kaynara Gumbargerie
John Hamilton
Thomas Howard
*John Jacobs
Juan Karanio
Kato
Okicirke Kichitoro

*Claud C. King
Kitaosajihi
*Charles F. Koch
Muskari Kotaro
Luis G. Manotanto
*Frank Mathews
*Jose Mendiolo
T. Mortimer
*Henry Perreira
*Charles Roeper
*Thomas Ryan
*Charles D. Sanford
Joe Santos
John Santos
*Antonio Silva
*Joe Silva
*Chris Starup
Charles Stewart
*C. Strelow

*W. H. Summers   Charles Visher
*Hugh N. Thyrd   Wakamatsie

VOYAGE 22 — December 3, 1896 — October 25, 1897
*John S. Layton, Master
*Horace F. Tower, 1st Mate
*Antonio Margarido, 2nd Mate
*Joe Avellar, 3rd Mate
*Honorio A. Martin, 4th Mate
 Emanuel Morgan, later mate
*Enos Aflague   Kemada Kuramruka
*Peder Andersen   *Peter Layton
*A. Andersson   Leander
*Carl Baptista   Peter Manscrieff
*Joe Basilleo   *Frank Mathews
*George Brown   *Jose Mendiola
*Jose Camacho   Morigo "Jap"
*Leonte de Cross   Yokohama Ohasuki
*Antonio de la Cruz   *Henry Olson
*Jose de los Santos   *Henry Perreia
*Louis Forrester   *George T. Samuel
*Thomas Gomes   Jose Santos
*Carl Greton   *John Stacy
*Ben Ignacio   *Chris Starup
 Ishitorationo   *W. H. Summers
*John Jacobs   *Peter Taitano
*W. Janman   Targuerlamarti
 Sakuminta Junkitan   *Hugh N. Thyrd
*Kaito   Chester Tokeka
*Jack Kelley   Frank Webber
*G. Kitooka   *John Williams
*O. Kitzi   Yokohama
*Charles F. Koch   *Charles Young

VOYAGE 23 — November 11, 1897 — October 28, 1898
*Thomas Scullun, Master
*Emanuel F. Morgan, 1st Mate

*George P. Christian, 2nd Mate

*Honorio A. Martin, 3rd Mate

*Joseph Thurston, 4th Mate

*Enos Aflague   *Joaquin Materne

*Peder Andersen   *Frank Mathews

*Joseph Avellar   *Fidel Morris

*J. F. Bartlett   Nanuilet

*Carl Baptista   K. Ozaki

 Joe Basilleo   *Jose Pangelino

*Fred J. Brown   *Lino Patricio

 George Brown   Joe Perado

*Torore Bue   *John Santos

 Antone Costa   *Jose Santos

*Cozaki   George Smith

 Cako Crouse   *W. H. Summers

 Joaquin de la Cruz   *Pedro Taitano

*Jose de los Santos   Takashasha (died)

*John Dooley   *Ernest Thompson

*Henry Gomes   Lewis Thurston

*Carl Greton   *W. Turner

*Charles F. Koch   *Koto Walamack

*Peter Layton   *Frank Webber

*James McCormick   *Charley Wills

 Robert F. Marshall   Osado Yoskisuku

VOYAGE 24 — November 26, 1898 — November 2, 1899

*Thomas Scullun, Master

*Emanuel F. Morgan, 1st Mate

*George P. Christian, 2nd Mate

*Honorio A. Martin, 3rd Mate

*Joseph Thurston, 4th Mate

*Enos Aflague   *Joe Cruz

*Peder Andersen   *Joaquin de la Cruz

 Joaquin Arriolo   *Jose de la Cruz

*Joe Avellar   Bread Fruit

*Mark M. Carroll   *Charles Gilmette

*Cozaki   *Henry Gomes

*Carl Greton

Frank Islida

*Charles F. Koch

*Peter Layton

Joe Lesama

*James McCormick

*James McGregor

*Joaquin Materne

*Frank Mathews

*Jose Mendiola

*Dennis Moran

*Fidel Morris

Antonio Pangalina

Venison Pangalina

*Joe Pangalino

*Lino Patricio

*Juan Perez

Joaquin Polio

*Robert Ritter

*John Rosario

*John Santos

*Jose Santos

*J. Schaffer

*George Smith

*Jose M. Souza

*W. H. Summers

*Thomas W. Swain

*Jose Tagnata

*Peter Taitano

Francisco Tenorio

*Luis Thurston

Sisoki Torria

*Frank Webber

*Osada Yashiske

VOYAGE 25 — December 7, 1899 — October 29, 1900

*Thomas Scullun, Master

*Emanuel F. Morgan, 1st Mate

*George P. Christian, 2nd Mate

*Honorio A. Martin, 3rd Mate

*Joseph Thurston, 4th Mate

*Peder Andersen

*Joaquin Arriolo

*Jose Augustine

*W. A. Bailey

*Nelson G. Carleton

*Henry Corte

*John de Castro

*Joaquin de la Cruz

Gregorio de la Rama

*Philip Domingo

*John Gareno

*W. L. Hall

W. H. Johnson

*H. Lahmeyer

*Ernest Lemans

John Lewin

*James McCormick

*Joaquin Materne

*Frank Mathews

*Dennis Moran

*Fidel Morris

*Joaquin Palacio

*Ben Pangalino

Joe Pangalino

*Antonio Pangeliman

*Frank Patrico

*Lino Patricio
*Juan Perez
 Frank Peterson
 Ben Petra
 Ben Regas
*John Rosario
*Sam Rotama
*Ben Santos
*John Santos
*Jose Santos
*W. E. Sloat

*George P. Smith
*Ernest Sornano
*Thomas Stokes
*Charlie Strelow
*W. H. Summers
*Thomas W. Swain
*Joken Tenorio
*C. M. Tower
*Frank Webber
*Ben Whitney

VOYAGE 26 — November 22, 1900 — October 29, 1901

*James A. M. Earle, Master
*George F. Allen, 1st Mate
*George P. Christian, 2nd Mate
*Honorio A. Martin, 3rd Mate
*Joseph Thurston, 4th Mate
*Thomas W. Swain, 5th Mate

*Joaquin Arriolo
*Fred Britton
*John Castro
*Christ Christian
*Manuel Claudina
*H. Corte
*Philip Domingo
*Adolphus F. Grose
*Jerry Guam
*Paul Hackentroich
*Otto Hoffman
*H. H. Johnson
*W. F. Lincoln
*John Lopes
*Manuel Lopes
*James McCormick
*Frank Mathews

*Fidel Morris
*Thomas Oliveira
*Lino Patricio
*John Pereira
*Mike Roderick
*Vicente Sales
*Ben Santos
*John Santos
*Manuel Silvia
*Thomas Stokes
*W. H. Summers
*Rehina Tehada
*C. M. Tower
*John Waller
*Frank Webber
*J. A. Welch

VOYAGE 27 — November 27, 1901 — October 28, 1902

*Thomas Scullun, Master
*Emanuel F. Morgan, 1st Mate
*Charles D. Sanford, 2nd Mate
*Joseph Thurston, 3rd Mate
*C. M. Tower, 4th Mate

*C. E. Allen
*Peder Andersen
*Antone Bartholdo
*R. W. Black
*George G. Christian
*George P. Christian
*Manuel Claudina
*John de Castro
*Fred Ellingsen
*Lonnie Harper
*H. H. Johnson
*John Lewin
*Nelson Lambert
*John Lopes
*Manuel Lopez
*James McCormick
*Jose Mendiola
*Frank Miller
*H. D. Morton

*C. Mullaney
*Thomas Oliveira
*L. B. Palmer
*Jose Pagalino
*Ben Pangaline
*Jerry Pangaline
*John Pereira
*John Peres
*John Peterson
 Harry Puiglapp
 Isaac Puiglapp
 Jack Puiglapp
 Tom Puiglapp
*Vicente Sales
*Ben Santos
*Thomas Stokes
*Charles Strellow
*Frank Webber
*Frank Wilson

VOYAGE 28 — November 20, 1902 — October 27, 1903

*James A. M. Earle, Master
*Emanuel F. Morgan, 1st Mate
*George P. Christian, 2nd Mate
*Joseph Thurston, 3rd Mate
*John Pereira, 4th Mate

*Peder Andersen
*William Barrows
*Antone Bartoldi
*Walter Bechtel
*Manuel Claudina

*Ben Cruz
*Antone M. Eriss
*M. Flaherty
 J. Furkrmeta
*Nicholas Gellers

*Manuel Gonsalves
*Devol Hotchkiss
 Kido
*James Kilpatrick
*John Lewin
*Conrad Look
*John Lopes
*Manuel Lopez
 Mantero
*James McNeil
*Jose Mendiola
*H. D. Morton
 Yorchiro Okuyama
*Thomas Oliveira
*H. A. Pearey

*John Peterson
*Isaac Puilap
*Tom Puilap
*Pedro Quantillinia
 O. Rabayoski
*Clarence Reynolds
*Charles D. Sanford
*Bartolo Santos
*Manuel Silvia
*Jose M. Souza
*George W. Stratton
 W. Kuchi Tachichi
*Leno Tehada
*Frank Webber

VOYAGE 29 — November 18, 1903 — October 31, 1904

*James A. M. Earle, Master
*Charles A. Sparks, 1st Mate
*George P. Christian, 2nd Mate
*Joseph Thurston, 3rd Mate
*R. L. McLachlan, 4th Mate
*Jose M. Souza, 5th Mate
*Peder Andersen
*John Anderson
*H. A. Aurel
*William Barrows
*Arthur Biddle
*R. L. Chambers
*Manuel Claudina
*Jose de Castro
*A. Ekstrom
*Edward Faerber
*Nicholas Gellers
*Manuel Gonsalves
*E. Grundahl
*Eddie Hogan

 Asay Jap
 Kohara Jap
*B. A. Jones
*Adolf Koch
*Charles Kopatz
*Richard Ludwig
*John Lewin
*Conrad Look
*John Lopes
*James McConnell
*James McNeil
*H. D. Morton
*John Nusal
*Thomas Oliveira

*Jose Penero

*Peter Quintinalla

*James Russell

 Matoki Sakichi

*John T. Short

*Manuel Silvia

 Sato Spika

*Samuel Stein

*George W. Stratton

*John A. Taylor

 Sato Tomachichi

*Frank Webber

 Yamda Yakukicha

 Kikuchi Yoshimatuski

VOYAGE 30 — November 25, 1904 — June 12, 1906

*Edwin J. Reed, Master

*Emanuel F. Morgan, 1st Mate

(No 2nd mate listed)

*John Pereira, 3rd Mate

*Antone J. Alameda, 4th Mate

*Antone Silva, 5th Mate

 Jose L. Alameda

 Juan Arbares

*William Barrows

*Fred Borneman

*J. B. Brown

*Louis Dablien

*Jesus da la Cruz

 Centehan A. Faria

*Charles A. Fisher

 Ernest Getten

*Manuel Gonsalves

 Norman A. Graves

*Frank Greene

*E. Gumdhal

 Allyne Haynes

*Benjamin A. Jones

*Charles King

 Adolph Koch

*Herman Larson

*Richard Ludwig

 Terehu Maracaro

*H. D. Morton

*Antone Nicholas

 Papa

 Tahuroa Peck

*Paul Rasmussen

 Juan P. Roderigues

*James Rodgers

*Fred Rodman

*Manuel Rosa

 H. Rose

*Jose Rose

*James Russell

*John Starr

*Samuel Stein

*Harvard Stone

*George W. Stratton

 Tuna A. Tauna

 Cenaria Tessier

 Pahero A. Tuania

 Mahuria A. Vehuation

*T. Watson

*Frank Webber

VOYAGE 31 — August 11, 1906 — July 4, 1908

James A. M. Earle, Master,
    resigned
Hiram Nye, Master, succeeding
*A. Judson James, 1st Mate, discharged
*George P. Christian, 2nd Mate
Frank J. Almeida, 2nd Mate, succeeding
*John Pereira, 3rd Mate
*Antone J. Alameda, 4th Mate

James Alick
Pedro S. Almeida
*Joseph Beetham
*Joseph Briggs
*Arthur Bowers
*William H. T. Broadway
*John Brooks
Andrade D. Costa
*Joe Cruz
Joao da Rocha
Jose F. da Santos
*Antonio G. de Azevada
Victorino de Sousa
*Manuel de Rozario
*Henry V. Doherty
Honor E. Earle (Master's wife)
*Frank English
*John Gilbert
Robert T. Goodsall
James Harry
*Herbert C. Huchins
*Charles Johnson
Wesley Lowe
*Terehu Maracaro

*John Mars
J. J. Morrissey
*H. D. Morton
*William T. Neville
*Antone Nicholas
*Edward Outerbridges
*Edward Osborn
*John Peck
Francis Pereira
*William Peters
*Papau Piare
*Paul Rasmussen
*Joaquin Rosa
*Manuel Rosa
Fred Shore
*Harry Stein
*John Stevens
*Edward G. Thayer
*Henry Thompson
*Walter Thompson
David Wake
*Frank Webber
Richard Woods

VOYAGE 32 — September 2, 1908 — September 12, 1910

Arthur O. Gibbons, Master, ill,
    left vessel

*Charles S. Church, Relieving
   Master
J. J. Senna, 1st Mate, found
   insane, discharged
Joseph Roderick, 1st Mate,
   discharged
*Joseph Thurston, 2nd Mate
*Nicholas Francis, 3rd Mate,
   later 1st Mate

*James Alick	*Joseph King
*Thomas H. Bess	*Alfred Lopez
*Jose Borja	*John Lopez
William H. Brush	*Terehu Maracaro
*H. Carston	*Theodore Monteiro
*George P. Christian	*H. D. Morton
*Joe Cruz	*Antone Nichols
Jose da Costa	Benjamin Patricia
*Joao da Rocha	*John Peck
*Mathew Deas	*Paulo Rames
*Victorino de Sousa	*Paul Rasmussen
*Manuel dos Reis	*Antonio Rosa
*Henry Doyle	*Enaas Rosa
Wilfred N. Francis	*Joaquin Rosa
*Justa M. Ganetti	*Manuel Rozario
*Ramon Garido	*Pedro Silva
William Haggie	John Soares
Louis Hansen	Domingo Sousa (stowaway)
*James Harry	*Joseph Thomas
Robert Holmes	*Frank Webber
Peter Jackson	*William Wilson
*Charles Johnson	

VOYAGE 33 — May 10, 1911 — August 9, 1913
*Charles S. Church, Master
*William H. Griffiths, 1st Mate
*George P. Christian, 2nd Mate
*Thomas Stokes, 3rd Mate

*Shadrach D. Tilton, 4th Mate

Manuel Almeda	Edward Johnson
*Peder Andersen	Harold Johnson
A. P. Avila	Teddy Kanaka
*Arthur Barnes	*Phillip Lelle
*Clayton H. Bills	Victor D. Lopez
*Jose Borja	Jose Machado
William Boucher	*Joseph F. McDonald
*James A. Boyd	*Jack J. Merrill
John Brazil	*Herbert Muncey
*Joseph Byrnes	*John T. O'Brien
James Ceasar	Antonio Pangalinam
*Charlotte E. Church	John Peck
(Master's wife and Assistant	*Manuel Pina
Navigator)	Pigarto Prieto
*Manuel Claudina	M. J. Reis
*Daniel J. Conway	*Enaas Rosa
Joe Cruz	Jose Santos
M. M. Cruz	*Frank Sears
*John W. Dawson	Frederick Scott
*Henry Doyle	*Joseph Shea
*William J. Drohan	Frank Silva
*Charles Edwards	Joe Silvia
Ernest	M. J. Silvia
M. A. Francis	M. Soares
*William Gillam	Domingo Sousa
*Bernard Gomes	*Manuel A. Tegue
J. J. Gomes	Ernst C. Thomas
*Manuel J. Gomez	*Walter J. Tiplow
*Alvan Goodman	*Ira Tucker
Robert Holmes	*Frank Williams
Peter Jackson	Joseph Wing
Isaac L. Joab, died at sea	Frederick Yar

VOYAGE 34 — September 5, 1916 — October 23, 1917
*Benjamin D. Cleveland, Master
*John D. Lopes, 1st Mate

*John Leamba, 2nd Mate
*Walter Thompson, 3rd Mate

*Joe Almeda
*Lewis F. Bond
*Arthur Bowers
*Fred I. Brigham
*James E. Clarke
*Benjamin W. Cleveland
*John Culgin
*Antonio Fonseca
*Charles Harris
*Arthur Jackson
*Edward Jon
*Howard McCormick

*Frank McLellan
*Frank Matley
*Antone Montario
*Edward W. Morse II
*Henry Murphy
*Dan O'Connor
*Frank Payzant
*Bert Smith
*Sylvester L. Souza
*Joseph Thomas
*Earle Wentworth
*Edward Winslow

VOYAGE 35 — July 16, 1918 — September 7, 1919

*Joseph F. Edwards, Master
*Theophilo M. Freitas, Mate

*Frank Almeda
*John V. Almeida
*Antonio Andreade
*Joao J. Aniseto
*Jacinto Costa
*Harry Cruse
*Joao B. Duarte
*Manuel Flora
*Benjamin Freitas
*Pedro Freitas
*Antonio R. Gomes
*William W. Higginbotham

*Manuel D. Jackson
*William Knowles, Jr.
*Jose F. Lopez
*Nahum Nickelson II
*Manuel Oliveira
*Manuel Ramos
*Antonio J. Rosa
*Joe Santos
*Jose A. Soares
*Joseph Stephenson
*Paul Tarvas
*Harold E. Tilton

VOYAGE 36 — October 18, 1919 — July 16, 1920

*Joseph F. Edwards, Master
*Peter B. Alves, 1st Mate
*Benjamin Freitas, 2nd Mate
*Thomas Lima, 3rd Mate

*Frank W. Almeda
*John J. Amigo

*Henry Correa
*Bartholome J. Encainede

*Antonio M. Freitas
*Pedro A. Freitas
*Manuel Gomes
*Silveiro Lopes
*Miguel Lopes
*Joao P. Manteir
*Dennis Pena

*Joao Ramos
*Manuel J. Rozario
*Luis M. Silva
*Vincente Silva
*Nicolau Talantino
*Jules Tavares

VOYAGE 37 — September 9, 1920 — May 28, 1921

*John Gonsalves, Master
*Frank M. Freitas, 1st Mate
*Antonio Tavares, 2nd Mate
*Frank Spencer, 3rd Mate
*Antonio D. Soares, 4th Mate

*Jose Barros
*Joe Cruize
*Nicolas A. Cruze
*Manuel J. Fonseca
*Antonio Gomes
*Antonio M. Lopes
*Eugenio P. Lopes
*M. Lopes
*Antonio S. Monteiro
*D. Pina

*Edward Ramos
*John A. Reis
*Manuel Rosario
*Louis Santos
*Micke Silva
*Mario R. Soares
*Pedro S. Soares
*Valentine Soares
*Jose Tavars

Logbooks

THIS listing contains forty-seven known official logbooks, abstracts and private journals for the whaleship *Charles W. Morgan.* Reading from left to right in columns are the voyage number, dates of the voyage, keeper of the volume, if known, and its location. Periods covered vary from four days to five years.

1.	1841–1845	James C. Osborn	Duke's County Historical Society
		James C. Osborn Abstract	G. W. Blunt White Library National Archives
2.	1845–1848	Frederick Vincent	Providence Public Library
		Unknown Abstract	G. W. Blunt White Library National Archives
3.	1849–1853	Nelson Cole Haley	G. W. Blunt White Library
5.	1856–1859	Unknown	Old Dartmouth Historical Society
		Unknown	Old Dartmouth Historical Society
6.	1859–1863	James A. Hamilton	G. W. Blunt White Library
7.	1863–1867	Unknown	New Bedford Free Public Library
		Unknown	New Bedford Free Public Library
		Charles W. Chace	G. W. Blunt White Library
8.	1867–1871	Alvan H. Davis	G. W. Blunt White Library
9.	1871–1874	Unknown	New Bedford Free Public Library
		Hiram Look	G. W. Blunt White Library
10.	1875–1878	Charles L. Willis	Providence Public Library
11.	1878–1881	William S. Baker	Barbara Johnson Collection
		Unknown	Old Dartmouth Historical Society

12.	1881–1886	Unknown	G. W. Blunt White Library
		Unknown	Providence Public Library
15.	1888–1889	Unknown	G. W. Blunt White Library
17.	1890–1891	James A. M. Earle	Private Collector
18.	1891–1892	James A. M. Earle	Private Collector
20.	1893–1895	Unknown	New Bedford Free Public Library
22.	1896–1897	Antonio Margarido	Private Collector
23.	1897–1898	Emanuel F. Morgan	G. W. Blunt White Library
26.	1900–1901	Unknown	New Bedford Free Public Library
27.	1901–1902	Emanuel F. Morgan	G. W. Blunt White Library
28.	1902–1903	Emanuel F. Morgan	G. W. Blunt White Library
29.	1903–1904	Unknown	New Bedford Free Public Library
30.	1904–1906	Unknown	New Bedford Free Public Library
31.	1906–1908	Unknown	G. W. Blunt White Library
		Unknown	New Bedford Free Public Library
		Arthur O. Gibbons	Sterling Library, Yale University
32.	1908–1910	Unknown	New Bedford Free Public Library
		Charlotte Church	G. W. Blunt White Library
33.	1911–1913	Unknown	Barbara Johnson Collection
		William H. Griffiths	G. W. Blunt White Library
		William H. Griffiths	G. W. Blunt White Library
34.	1916–1917	Benjamin D. Cleveland	G. W. Blunt White Library
		John D. Lopes	G. W. Blunt White Library
35.	1918–1919	Unknown	Old Dartmouth Historical Society
		Unknown	G. W. Blunt White Library
36.	1919–1920	Joseph F. Edwards	Kendall Whaling Museum
37.	1920–1921	Unknown	Old Dartmouth Historical Society
		Unknown	G. W. Blunt White Library

Summary of Voyages

Whaling Ship
Charles W. Morgan

THE following summary of voyages and gross value of cargoes was taken from information bulletins compiled by Dr. Charles R. Schultz and members of the staff of the G. W. Blunt White Library of The Marine Historical Association, Incorporated.

Voyage # 1. Sailed from New Bedford September 6, 1841
  Thomas A. Norton, Master; Charles W. Morgan et al.,
   owners
  Returned to New Bedford January 1, 1845
  Value of cargo, $56,068
Voyage # 2. Sailed from New Bedford June 10, 1845
  John D. Samson, Master; Charles W. Morgan et al., owners
  Returned to New Bedford December 9, 1848
  Value of cargo, $69,394.50
Voyage # 3. Sailed from New Bedford June 5, 1849
  John D. Samson, Master; Edward M. Robinson et al., owners
  Returned to New Bedford May 27, 1853
  Value of cargo, $44,138.75
Voyage # 4. Sailed September 20, 1853
  Tristam P. Ripley, Master; I. Howland, Jr. & Co., agents

Returned to New Bedford April 27, 1856
Value of cargo, $76,183.64

Voyage # 5. Sailed from New Bedford September 15, 1856
Thomas N. Fisher, Master; I. Howland, Jr. & Co., agents
Returned to New Bedford April 16, 1859
Value of cargo, $62,720.84

Voyage # 6. Sailed from New Bedford October 4, 1859
James A. Hamilton, Master; I. Howland, Jr. & Co., agents
Returned to New Bedford May 12, 1863
Value of cargo, $165,405.74

Voyage # 7. Sailed from New Bedford December 1, 1863
Thomas C. Landers, Master; J. & W. R. Wing, owners
Returned to New Bedford June 12, 1867
Value of cargo, $50,014.13

Voyage # 8. Now rerigged as a bark and remeasured to register 313.75
tons
Sailed from New Bedford July 17, 1867
George Athearn, Master; J. & W. R. Wing, owners
Returned to New Bedford August 16, 1871
Value of cargo, $49,722.54

Voyage # 9. Sailed from New Bedford September 26, 1871
John M. Tinkham, Master; J. & W. R. Wing, owners
Returned to New Bedford October 31, 1874
Value of cargo, $78,982.40

Voyage #10. Sailed from New Bedford April 23, 1875
Same master and owners
Returned to New Bedford May 17, 1878
Value of cargo, $25,880.40

Voyage #11. Sailed from New Bedford July 17, 1878
T. L. Ellis, Master; same owners
Returned to New Bedford May 11, 1881
Value of cargo, $52,483.60

Voyage #12. Sailed from New Bedford July 13, 1881
Charles F. Keith, Master; same owners
Returned to New Bedford June 18, 1886
Value of cargo, $26,545.05

Voyage #13. Sailed from New Bedford October 6, 1886

George A. Smith, Master; same owners
Returned to San Francisco November 4, 1887
Value of cargo, $50,620.92

Voyage #14. Sailed from San Francisco December 3, 1887
Same master and owners
Returned to San Francisco November 5, 1888
Value of cargo, $19,831.69

Voyage #15. Sailed from San Francisco November 26, 1888
John S. Layton, Master; same owners
Returned to San Francisco October 27, 1889
Value of cargo, $28,182

Voyage #16. Sailed from San Francisco December 5, 1889
Same master and owners
Returned to San Francisco November 8, 1890
Value of cargo, $13,725.20

Voyage #17. Sailed from San Francisco December 2, 1890
James A. M. Earle, Master; same owners
Returned to San Francisco October 31, 1891
Value of cargo, $36,992.50

Voyage #18. Sailed from San Francisco November 24, 1891
Same master and owners
Returned to San Francisco November 7, 1892
Value of cargo, $15,241

Voyage #19. Sailed from San Francisco December 8, 1892
Same master and owners
Returned to San Francisco November 9, 1893
Value of cargo, $11,606.35

Voyage #20. Sailed from San Francisco December 6, 1893
Same master and owners
Returned to San Francisco November 5, 1895
Value of cargo, $42,640

Voyage #21. Sailed from San Francisco December 2, 1895
Same master and owners
Returned to San Francisco November 1, 1896
Value of cargo, $12,061.25

Voyage #22. Sailed from San Francisco December 3, 1896
John S. Layton, Master; same owners

Returned to San Francisco October 25, 1897
Value of cargo, $19,031.25

Voyage #23. Sailed from San Francisco November 11, 1897
Thomas Scullun, Master; same owners
Returned to San Francisco October 28, 1898
Value of cargo, $24,622.65

Voyage #24. Sailed from San Francisco November 26, 1898
Same master and owners
Returned to San Francisco November 2, 1899
Value of cargo, $25,933.50

Voyage #25. Sailed from San Francisco December 7, 1899
Same master and owners
Returned to San Francisco October 29, 1900
Value of cargo, $25,042.50

Voyage #26. Sailed from San Francisco November 22, 1900
James A. M. Earle, Master; same owners
Returned to San Francisco October 29, 1901
Value of cargo, $30,956.56

Voyage #27. Sailed from San Francisco November 27, 1901
Thomas Scullun, Master; same owners
Returned to San Francisco October 28, 1902
Value of cargo, $32,826.15

Voyage #28. Sailed from San Francisco November 20, 1902
James A. M. Earle, Master; same owners
Returned to San Francisco October 27, 1903
Value of cargo, $30,870

Voyage #29. Sailed from San Francisco November 18, 1903
Same master and owners
Returned to San Francisco October 31, 1904
Value of cargo, $23,814

Voyage #30. Sailed from San Francisco November 25, 1904
E. J. Reed, Master; same owners
Returned to New Bedford June 12, 1906
Value of cargo, $25,222.05

Voyage #31. Sailed from New Bedford August 11, 1906
James A. M. Earle, Master; same owners. Captain Hiram
Nye went out to South Africa to take over the bark when

Captain Earle resigned because of ill health
Returned to New Bedford July 4, 1908
Value of cargo, $24,900.75

Voyage #32. Sailed from New Bedford September 2, 1908
Arthur O. Gibbons, Master; same owners. Captain Charles S.
Church took over for latter part of voyage
Returned to New Bedford September 12, 1910
Value of cargo, $25,250.40

Voyage #33. Sailed from New Bedford May 10, 1911
Charles S. Church, Master; same owners
Returned to New Bedford August 9, 1913
Value of cargo, $44,225.76

Voyage #34. Sailed from New Bedford September 5, 1916
Benjamin D. Cleveland, Master and owner
Returned to New Bedford October 23, 1917
Value of cargo, $21,766.50

Voyage #35. Sailed from New Bedford July 16, 1918 (Hailing from
Provincetown)
Joseph D. Edwards, Master; John A. Cook, owner
Returned to New Bedford September 7, 1919
Value of cargo, $26,444.25

Voyage #36. Sailed from New Bedford October 18, 1919
Joseph F. Edwards, Master and part owner
Returned to New Bedford July 16, 1920
Value of cargo only $8,977.50

Voyage #37. Sailed from New Bedford September 9, 1920
John Gonsalves, Master; J. A. Cook, owner
Returned to Provincetown May 28, 1921 then to New Bedford
Value of cargo, $25,533.90

Glossary

BARK — A partially square-rigged sailing vessel, having three or more masts, square-rigged on all but the last mast which had fore and aft sails. All whaling barks were three-masted.

BATTEN SEAM — A form of small boat construction where plank are laid, edge to edge, the inside seam being covered full length by a batten of lighter material, the fastenings extending through both edges of batten and planking.

BEARERS — Timbers fastened to the side of the vessel and standing upright, two between each set of davits, to steady the boats resting on the cranes which pivot from the bearers.

BITTER END — The inboard end of any line.

BLUBBER — The fatty substances which encase the body of a whale. These range from several inches to a foot thick, depending upon the size of the whale. When cooked out in the big try kettles, the blubber gave out the oil much as if one were frying salt pork or bacon. The process was called "trying out," or more commonly, among whalemen, "boiling."

BOATHEADER — Usually the mate in charge, although occasionally a whaleboat was sent out in charge of an older, experienced boatsteerer and he was then designated as boatheader.

BOATSTEERER — He also served as harpooner, pulled the forward oar in a whaleboat and harpooned the whale. Once the job was done, he went aft and changed places with the mate (or boatheader as he was sometimes called) and steered the boat while the mate killed the whale with a lance.

BOWHEAD WHALE — A specie which abounds in the Bering Sea, in the Pacific, and off Spitzbergen and Greenland in the Atlantic.

BOX — A portion of the forward deck of a whaleboat, margined at the after end by the "clumsy cleat."

BOX WARP — Sometimes called the stray line. Part of the whale line coiled down in the "box" in the bow of the boat before passing out through the notched stem.

BREAKDOWN — As used here, means a general get-together with music, singing, dancing, etc.

CLUMSY CLEAT — A heavy wooden brace which extends across the after end of the foredeck in the bow of a whaleboat. It has a notch used by the harpooner to brace himself. Projecting up through it is the rod to take the forward hoisting ring or shackle. The kicking strap leads down through it and is knotted underneath.

COURSES — Lower square sail on each mast. Spoken of individually, the sail was often called by the name of the mast from which it was set. The *Morgan* set a foresail and mainsail (or forecourse and main course) and like many of the older ships did not set a sail from the mizzen yard.

CRANES — Hinged, triangular wooden brackets which swing into a horizontal position from the bearers. When the boat is hoisted in the davits from the water, it is set down on the cranes.

CRIMPS — Boarding house masters and agents for supplying crews in the later days of sailing ships. They maintained almost complete control over crews as soon as they appeared on the waterfront.

CUTTING IN — The process of cutting the blubber or fat away from the carcass of the whale as it lies in the water alongside the ship. Usually done by the mates who worked from a cutting stage rigged out over the side.

CUTTING SPADE — A tool shaped like a spade, 8″ or 10″ across and sharpened along the bottom edge for cutting blubber from the whale after it was alongside the ship.

CUTTING STAGE — A long, wooden staging, usually made up of two or three narrow planks to allow water to drain through and extending parallel to the side of the ship for about 12′ or more. It is held out from the side of the vessel by planks extended out at right angles and suspended by tackles and lashings from the rigging and rails. Iron stanchions hold a pole railing along the length of the staging, about waist high, and the mates, or those cutting in, leaned against this while wielding their cutting spades.

CUTTING TACKLE — The big tackles which are hooked or shackled into a chain or rope "necklace" around the mainmast head and used for hoisting in the blubber. The blocks are usually from 16″ to 20″ in size, with falls in proportion. There are several ways to rig cutting tackles but the most usual is to have double blocks at the lower end with hook or toggle and two single blocks aloft, since one part of the tackle leads off athwartship while the hauling part is led forward. There are also guy tackles leading to the foremast head to bring the tackles forward clear of the main yard and sail.

DAVITS — Heavy wooden timbers fastened to the sides of a whaler. The tops are steam bent in a semicircular fashion to form a projection. The top is slotted and fitted with sheaves or pulley wheels through which the rope falls are led to form tackles for hoisting the boats. The heavy wooden davits are the unique identifying mark of the whaler.

DRAWED — The whalemen's ungrammatical synonym for "drew." After a whale was harpooned, the harpoon sometimes pulled out and the whaleman's description was that he had "drawed his iron."

DROGUE — Usually a wooden platform about 2′–2½′ square, bridled from each corner with whale line. If a whale ran out all of the line in the tubs, the drogue was made fast to the bitter end of the second line and tossed overboard to further impede the whale's progress.

FALLS — The line used in making up a tackle. Boat falls were rove through sheaves in the davits with a good-sized double block being hooked into a hoisting ring at each end of the boats.

FATHOM — One fathom equals six feet.

FINBACK WHALE — A species usually taken along the coasts by small boat whalemen. Fairly common along the New England coast at one time.

FLUKE PIPE — A hawse hole, cut low through bulwark and plank-sheer, through which the fluke chain is led from the tail of the whale to the fluke bitt abreast of the foremast, on the starboard side only.

GALLEY OR GALLIED — To startle a whale and cause him to swim away before he (or she) can be harpooned.

Galley is also the compartment or deckhouse where all cooking is done.

GAMMING — When two whaling ships met at sea, if the weather was at all favorable, they hove to and some of the crew members visited back and forth. Captains' wives did so almost invariably.

GOOSE PEN — A watertight, boxlike structure built on deck on which the brick tryworks is set. It is kept filled with water when there is a fire in the tryworks to prevent the deck from being scorched or set afire.

GROUNDS — Areas in various seas and oceans where whales were plentiful.

GUNWALE — The rail or edge of an open boat.

HARPOONER — Synonymous with boatsteerer.

HAWSE HOLE — Oval-shaped cut through the bulwarks of a vessel into which is inserted and fastened an iron casting through which lines or chains are passed.

HEAVE SHORT — To take in all the anchor chain by pumping the windlass brakes.

HUMPBACK WHALE — A specie usually taken around the West Indies and the Cape Verde and Azores Islands in the Atlantic and off the West Coast of Central America in the Pacific; also off the lower California coast.

IRON — The whaleman's invariable name for a harpoon.

JACK — A piece of light timber, sawed down vertically to enable the outside legs to be spread by a dowel extending through all three legs transversely, thus making a rest for the two "working" harpoons. It passed downward through a cleat at the gunwale and projected above the gunwale about a foot. The two harpoons lay in it side by side, separated by the middle leg, their barbs or points resting forward in the box.

KICKING STRAP — A heavy piece of line made fast at each end through holes in the clumsy cleat and under which the whale line passes before being coiled down in the box.

LANDFALL — The first sight of land after a voyage or passage.

LAPSTREAK — A form of small boat construction where narrow, preferably full-length plank are lapped one over the other and fastened at close intervals along the edges.

LAY — Whalemen got their pay in the form of a lay or share in the proceeds of a catch, less certain expenses. Lays varied from 1/200 to 1/15, depending on the rank or experience of the men who received them, and were agreed upon before the voyage began.

LIGHT SAILS — Extra sails of lighter-weight canvas, set in addition to the working sails in lighter weather.

LUFF — To bring a sailing vessel up, bow into the wind, with sails shaking so that the vessel loses headway.

NANTUCKET SLEIGH RIDE — Whaleboat towed by a harpooned whale.

RIGHT WHALE — Specie found on both the Japan grounds and around New Zealand, but not usually on the equator.

ROYAL — The sail above the topgallant sail. Usually the uppermost sail on any mast, as few, if any whalers carried skysails.

SCRIMSHAW — A folk art practiced primarily by whalemen who used sperm whale teeth and whalebone to engrave pictures upon, or to make pie crimpers or other articles which they took home to their wives or sweethearts. Synonyms were scrimshon and scrimshander, as well as other variations of the word.

SCRIMSHONING — Working on scrimshaw. Other words meaning the same would be scrimshawing, scrimshandering, etc.

SHIP — As a specific designation of rig it meant a square-rigged sailing ship with three or more masts, square-rigged on all masts. Whalers were never more than three-masted. In generic terms, it could be used to speak of any large vessel.

SLIDE BOARDS — Light springy boards, about 8" to 10" wide, bent and fastened vertically to the side of the ship between the bearers or davits to hold the side of the whaleboat away and keep it from catching the gunwale on any projections.

SLOP CHEST — A supply of tobacco, clothes, sheath knives and sundries carried on board ship for the crew to purchase, the price being charged against their lay and settled up when they were paid off at the end of the voyage. The captain usually reaped the profits.

SOUND — When a whale was harpooned, he often dove and headed for the bottom. This was called "sounding."

SPERM WHALE — A specie which was generally found in warmer equatorial waters, but also ranged widely into both the North and South Atlantic and Pacific.

STOVE — Smashed, usually by a whale. A whale would often thrash around after being harpooned or lanced and in so doing damage or destroy the whaleboat. This would be spoken of as a "stove" boat.

STUDDING SAILS (stu'n's'ls to a seaman) — Extra light-weight sails set from the yardarms and sheeted to studding sail booms which slid outward from the yards through rings.

SULPHUR-BOTTOM WHALE — The largest specie of whale known. Taken in small numbers on no special grounds.

TONNAGE — A figure arrived at by computation, and based on an arbitrary formula, to be used in registering or documenting a vessel. It has nothing to do with weight, displacement, carrying capacity, etc.

TOPGALLANT MAST — The third section of mast above the deck from which was set not only the topgallant sail but the royal above it. Clipper ships sometimes set a skysail above the royal but few whalers did.

TOPSAILS — The next sail above the course on each mast. In the early days it was one large sail, but from the 1860s on was frequently divided into two sails and an extra yard or spar and became double topsails. Topsails were set from a yard or spar on the topmast, the first section of mast above the lower mast.

TRYWORKS — A structure built of bricks over a goose pen (which could be filled with water), on deck aft of the fore hatch. It was built around two large iron kettles in which the fat or blubber was cooked out to produce oil.

WHALE LINE — Often called tow line by whalemen; usually ¾″ long-fibered manila of the best grade. When breaking out a new coil, the line was led up through a temporary block aloft and thence down to the boatsteerer on deck to be carefully flemish-coiled into the line tub to prevent possible kinking.

WHIP — A line, usually rigged temporarily, which led through a block aloft and back to the deck again for hoisting lighter weights.

YARD — A spar to which was fastened the head or upper edge of a square sail and which was raised or lowered to set or take in sail.

Index

THE *Charles W. Morgan*

was composed in Linotype Garamond and Typo Script
display type. The typesetting and printing is
by Connecticut Printers, Inc. The edition was
bound by Complete Book Bindery.
Designed by Raymond M. Grimaila.

Mystic Seaport
THE MARINE HISTORICAL ASSOCIATION, INC.
Mystic, Connecticut